Memoirs of an Accidental Psychic

L. Duncan Hartgraves

Joshua Tree Publishing

• Chicago •

Memoirs of an Accidental Psychic

L. Duncan Hartgraves

Joshua Tree Publishing
• Chicago •
JoshuaTreePublishing.com

13-Digit ISBN: 978-1-956823-72-1

Cover & Image Credits: L. Duncan Hargraves.

Disclaimer:

Printed in the United States of America

Dedication

I dedicate this book to my family and most importantly, my passed family members. I know you are watching and smiling down on me.

Table of Contents

Picture taken during late Winter, near my home

Prologue

Blessings! So, I have been asked to write this by several devout fans. This is a compilation of many weird, exciting, bizarre, but true psychic/ghost phenomena. (And yes, these stories are 100% true!)

A lot of people wanna know how I came to understand my gifts and how I've dealt with it—and continue to deal with situations. I had a wise friend once tell me, "Remember to write from your heart." So, that is what I am doing.

Thirty years ago, I would have never dreamed in a million years that I would be a practicing psychic with millions of fans. I call myself psychic because that is a popular term, but I guess "seer" or "visionary" might be a better term. I also kinda like the word "mystic."

I know what I do comes from God. This has seemed to happen by accident, hence the name, *Memoirs of an Accidental Psychic*. I have to admit, though, that there are no such things as accidents, so in a way, the title is an oxymoron.

I never dreamed things would happen this way, that I'd be a practicing medium, that Jesus would appear to me and give me messages and predictions, or that I would be helping and supporting the spirituality of hundreds of thousands of people. Jesus told me in his messages, that at my core, I am a writer, so here we are. But as we all know, in the Age of Aquarius, things will happen that will blow our minds. And we can feel it. I know we CAN ALL FEEL it. It's in our faces; it's entwined in our souls. Our planet is evolving and so are we.

Parts of this were not easy. The bullying that I endured growing up has taken its toll, even today. It's funny how we never forget. I hope maybe by telling some of this, not only can you have a deeper understanding of the human condition, but maybe you will teach a little kindness to the next generation. Thinking of others should always be what propels you forward.

I have found throughout my life that whenever I try to do things for selfish reasons, I fall flat on my face. Whenever I do something to help others, that is where I am successful. I am always in service to you all. That is my purpose. I hope by reading this, it may help you in some way. I try hard to make it not just about me, but about you, too. When reading, I hope you relate this to your own life.

I guess you could consider this my memoir of my escapades and life as a psychic medium, herbalist, and hypnotist. I'll try to do this in chronological order, but some might be a tad moved around. I changed many of the names to protect the privacy of others.

I hope you love true ghost stories. As you will see, "things" seem to follow me around.

There are a lot of messages also. I receive messages from Angels, Jesus, and even aliens. (Yes, aliens believe in angels, Jesus and Source.) These messages are mostly at the end, as we begin the process of the Age of Aquarius.

I hope you like my stories. You may find some similarities to it in your own life. I tell the stories often, mostly on my podcast, *Metaphysical Meanderings*. I hope you can use some of this wisdom. This can also be considered a reference book also of some knowledge I've shared.

This book has been written just for you, wherever you are in your journey!

Enjoy!

Let me know; I do care.

Well at Least the Trauma Made Me Funny . . .

I came from a pretty traditional home with an older brother, mom, and dad, in a traditional Midwestern town in Wisconsin. My only difference was that my mom had a job. Back then, many moms still stayed home. I think that was what shaped me so much. I grew up fiercely independent and still am.

Initially, I was born early, and at the last minute. I was born on a Monday morning. The doctor told my mom to go to the hospital. The doctor wasn't in yet when she arrived but came in that morning. I was delivered in the morning at about 8:00 a.m.

When you are born is very important, morning, afternoon, or evening. It sets your circadian rhythms for the rest of your lives.

I was born in the morning, and I am at my very best at that time. Our birthdays are so important! I firmly believe that we plan the time and day. I knew that the doctor would deliver me then.

My delivery was an emergency. I was already getting sick. My mom had Toxemia, and it had already moved to the placenta. It was imperative that I would be born when I was. I was delivered by C-section over a month early. They gave me oxygen at birth, and it damaged my eyes. I've worn glasses since the age of four. I was already toxic and refused to eat. The hospital had to put a tube into my stomach to give me food.

My mom was a severe diabetic. My mom had lost an older brother at birth, so she was glad I was born alive. They told her I was a boy. She thought she had two sons.

Could you imagine her surprise when she opened my diaper!

My mom used to tell that story often. Maybe that is what made me into such a tom-boy. I've always felt that I have a lot of male energy, but I have both energies, depending on the situation. Everyone has some energy that is both male and female. I think my energy is very split between the two genders. While I love sports and competition, I love being a mom and grandma. Sometimes, though, even at a young age, I didn't like being a girl. I could see the inequalities even then. I also grew up and played with all boys, so the tomboy in me was well ingrained. I remember crying when I got my period at twelve.

In the 70s, "Women's Lib" was in its infancy. I remember watching the marches and the burning of bras. (Why bras, I'm not really sure; I REALLY need mine as I get older!)

Every feminist was labeled as domineering and angry, things women should NEVER be according to the norms of the society at that time. Back then, it was a horrible thing to be called a "feminist," but I was one, even at seven. I knew that I could do anything and be anything. I knew I was smart and could achieve things. I heard a phrase recently that resonates now as it did then and totally agree with it now:

"Feminism is the outrageous idea that women are equal human beings and should be treated as such."

My mother used to tell me as a kid that "men are better at everything than us."

Geez, misogyny is so ingrained. I'd argue and argue. I knew in my heart that in no way I was inferior. Some of my family members even tried to shut me up, which made me even louder. I kind of think that I am such a strong woman because of my mother telling me these things. I grew up rebelling against the system. I grew up refusing to be a "polite" woman.

Maybe that was why I ended up with three daughters and two granddaughters. I am here to support and guide other women. I truly feel that is what really is wrong with our society today. We, as women, do not support and celebrate each other. Misogyny is so ingrained in our society, that we are victims at our cores.

Why NOT be happy for other women? Why NOT celebrate a strong, courageous woman? Why do we women think it will somehow take away from us somehow? What the problem is that we have been programmed to fight amongst ourselves to keep us divided.

I truly believe that there **is** no way on God's green Earth that I am inferior to any man. Any man who feels that way has a frail male ego and really needs to look at themselves and the belief system that taught them that. A secure male will realize that all humans are equal with gifts and talents from God. That is a true man in my book. My husband has never stood in my way, and the other man in my life always encouraged me.

My dad was the opposite of my mom. While my mom supported me, my dad encouraged me. He always had faith in me. I identified greatly with him. He was one of the smartest people I ever met. He became an electrical engineer without a degree and worked on the electrical panels on one of the Apollo missions to the moon. I looked up to him, even with his demons. While he wasn't the most ambitious man, he taught me to stick with what you are good at. My parent's marriage wasn't that great, but they stayed married until the end. My dad used to say, "You work hard or you work smart. You don't do both."

Unfortunately, my dad was an alcoholic. Looking back now, I think he may have been mildly bi-polar. He was sent away when I was three to "dry out." He never took another drink. He had an addictive personality, though. If it wasn't alcohol, it was Diet Coke, or archery, or a gambling. He always became obsessed with something.

I remember clearly when he came home after being put away. My grandparents bought me and my brother toys. I got a doll (which I didn't like), and my brother got a barn and farm set that I really wanted. (I was an animal and farm lover even then!) My dad used to call me "sissy." He's a guide now that he's gone and visits on occasion.

My dad chose my name. Supposedly, he had been watching a movie with Lana Turner, Kirk Douglas, and Dana Andrews in it. That's how my name was chosen, as well as my siblings. My mom wanted to name me Valerie (I so don't seem like a Valerie).

We really do choose our own names. We kinda give our parents the idea. I think I chose well, except for the fact many people pronounce my name wrong. It's Laaana, like apple, not Lahna. Actually, Lana is a very feminine name, but people have actually researched my name and found that women named Lana are often tomboys and grow up to be attractive and go-getters.

I am one of these people who can remember way back in my life. My farthest back memory was that I must've been around a year and a half old. I can remember being in diapers and getting moved out of my crib. I remember it all clearly. It was a Saturday. My mom told me I was moving to a "big girl's bed."

I'm not sure why memory is so good. I often wonder if this has something to do with my abilities. I've noticed throughout my experiences that many children who remember their past lives also have intense psychic ability also. Think back and see how far you can remember. Most people can't remember much. All I know is that I remember a lot from my childhood before I started school.

Thinking back, I was only two or three, but TV was my first babysitter; the myriad of other adults who watched me came second. I remember *Captain Kangaroo*, reruns of *The Beverly Hillbillies* and *Gilligan's Island*. I guess I was a typical American kid being entertained by electronics even then.

When I wasn't watching TV, I was outside. I remember once when it was finally able to play outside without a coat. That was usual in May and the start of summer. That was a BIG deal; Wisconsin winters were brutal.

It seemed like summers went on forever. Time always seemed to creep, but I think that's the way it is for all kids. Now time flies. All of this just seemed like yesterday.

Being outside was my ultimate joy as it is now. Even today, if I could live in a tent year-round, I'm totally fine with that. I was lucky enough to have about an acre to roam around, with pastures and trails adjacent. Back then, it was normal to let a three- or four-year-old play by themselves, running, jumping and playing with rocks. I loved my time alone; I still do. But I remember climbing trees and digging in the dirt. And by-the-way, I still love it. If you wanna do something soulful, go dig in the dirt or hug a tree. Studies even prove how relaxing it is. Yes, nature and animals are my passion.

Horses are my true love. I'm not sure, but I think my love of horses is genetic. I realize now that there is much more to it than that. It's locked in the cells from genetics and past-life memories.

My father came from a family of horse trainers, farriers, and racers. He spent his whole life in the horse barns. He told me he learned how to crawl underneath a racehorse named "King Lear." He just never took to horses like I did, even though my grandpa did.

My first words were mommy, daddy, and gee-go (what I called horses). My parents thought it was cute but couldn't figure out why I used that word. My mom used to say that if I even saw a horse while riding in the car, I would scream and cry "geego." I always wondered why. As I was researching for this memoir, I decided to look up information. What I got was incredible.

First of all, the word gee-gee is a term used for horses in England by children. I am mostly Scott's Irish, so maybe that's where it came from, so I thought. Maybe it's genetic; we do inherit things from our families, but oh, no, it gets better than that.

I have always been attracted to the Native American culture. My first bike I rode, I pretended it was a horse. I used to pretend I owned a teepee and pulled my blankets up using a tree branch. Was this also ancestral? Just a year ago I found out that I was actually Native

American. My 6th great mother (yeah, a long time ago!) was a Shawnee named Minta Straighttail, and she was the aunt of Tecumseh.

As for me, I didn't realize until many years later when I did Past-Life Regression, that not only was I Native American many times, but also a horse breeder of a now extinct type of pony, closely related to what I think is the Nokota Horse (I think it was an Appaloosa/Paint cross of some type).

I do not remember calling horses Gee-goes.

By the time I was three or so, I called them horsies. As I did my research, I found that a dialect of Lakota Sioux used a word similar to what sounded like the corrupted word '"gee-go" for horse. It made me shudder. It hit me seriously, like a brick between my eyes. I was doing something from my past-life. It all made sense.

Ask your parents next time you see them or a family member if you ever said or did anything strange like that. I bet you'd be surprised. What I've found is that many children say or do something like this but don't remember it. The signs are just the same.

Remember, there is more to our story. Our ancestors can also often give us a piece of their life experiences, so these memories can be inherited. I inherited the love of horses that was stored in my DNA, combined with a past-life. Many studies have proven that familial trauma is real also.

Epigenetics is the study of how our genes are turned on or off by things other than DNA. These changes are sometimes passed to our children. There is a famous study about how Holocaust survivor's children suffered from increased stress hormones and stress-related disorders. Some speculate that even culturally, we sometimes do things much like our ancestors. No wonder why we are so screwed up!

Ever develop a sudden fear that you never had before? Maybe something like at twenty-seven, you suddenly developed a sudden fear of water? You probably drowned at the age of twenty-seven, or a family member did, and—your cells are storing the information. The best way to address this trauma is through Past-Life Regression, which helps release this information and heal it.

As for familial trauma passed down, there are several ways of releasing things. Epigenetic Healing is one. It helps you release the negative patterns inherited within families. I think the best way, though, of dealing with cellular trauma is Past-Life Regression.

If you've never had Past-Life Regression, I highly suggest finding a good, certified hypnotherapist. It will change your life. You remember people, places, and events and synthesize them back into your life. You start even recognizing people from your current life that you knew in other lives. It's wild! Funny thing is, when you start recognizing people, you can see in their eyes that they recognize you back!

It's sometimes hard to tell where the trauma originated, but usually it's primarily coming from a past-life. Either way, it's a mystery. For past-lives we often block the information. It's simply forgotten subconsciously, but our SOUL knows. It knows everything.

Why do we forget or block the information?

What I think happens and why we forget these past lives is because:

1. We are taught at about the age of five to seven in many parts of the world, that past lives don't exist, and people will think we're crazy, or . . .

2. We may have had severe trauma and purposely try to forget, or . . .

3. We are disconnected with who we are by pressures from society or parents who push their agendas on us.

What I think is happening, simply put, is that our subconscious has become disconnected from our soul. It knows the Akashic records (more about that later). Because of outside forces or trauma, we have forgotten who we are.

My middle daughter told me something quite interesting like this one day. She was about three, and she told me something strange when I was combing her hair one day. She told me she had been a fireman. I was a little surprised, and I asked her for more info. She proceeded to tell me about her tall boots, and the coat she wore. And then out of the clear blue, she got a little sad and said, 'But then I retired."

I was astounded. How would a three-year-old know what retirement was? So, I then asked her when did this happen?

"You KNOW, not now, BEFORE now." She looked at me in an irritated way.

She doesn't remember saying any of this today.

My youngest daughter used to go to Florida a lot to stay with her grandparents. One summer she came home after being gone for a few weeks and couldn't understand that her parent's names were Dan and Lana. She argued with us that they were George and Mary for the rest of the vacation.

My oldest granddaughter when she was three told me one day that her "other grandma" was mean to her and threw her in the trash.

"Not you grandma, my grandma before," she told me. "She lived in a big city, and she died." She went into great detail. She remembers nothing about it now.

Why is it that we remember until about the age of four? Just like I said, there are a few reasons, but we have leftover residue from the past-life and are assimilating into this one. Trust me, your soul knows and holds onto it. You just aren't always aware of it. But sometimes it shows up like gee-go did for me. Sometimes, there are things from many multiple lives, also.

Pay attention to themes in your life, too. A lot of times themes are repeated patterns from other lives. Past-Life Regression did help me get rid of most of my trauma. I am now a weather spotter and have had weight loss surgery! You can break these patterns if you are aware. And if you are wondering, yes, these traumas can be healed.

To heal these negative memories (especially a death in a past-lifetime) is to tell your soul and your cells that you are not going to die that way again. (The chances, right?) Do this before you go to bed for several weeks, and eventually, your cells and your soul will let go.

Doing this before sleeping is a great way to access your subconscious and connect it to your soul. For me, I told myself that I would not die in a tornado, and that I wouldn't starve to death, and over the years, like I said, it diminished. If it doesn't happen right away, don't be discouraged; be patient with yourself. At least there was an explanation now. Past-Life Regression is truly healing.

Now returning to my five-year-old self, I was a very healthy kid and kinda learned at a young age to take care of myself. Since one of my brothers was stillborn, and another almost died, I was the least of my mom's worries. Maybe that was why my mother and grandmother favored my brother so heavily over me. I didn't need their help. This could've been my astrological chart (Sagittarians are notoriously very independent), or from a past-life, no one will ever know, but even now, I have trouble letting people help me.

It's good that I was so independent. I had a slew of babysitters throughout my years while my mom worked. Some young, some old. I remember my mom paying twenty-five dollars per week, which were good wages back then.

I'll never forget one. Crazy Mrs. Smith was what we used to call her. She was an older lady who lived down the street from us. She told us one time that as a kid, John Dillinger robbed the bank in town, and made her stand on the running boards of his car so he could get outta town without being shot. (Nobody would've shot at a kid). No one ever believed her. She used to tell all kinds of stories, the odder the better. It wasn't until many years later, we found out this was true (only we didn't really know which gangster did it for sure).

I didn't always believe everything she said and was discerning even at the age of four. One day, she said a lady had her arm hanging out of the window of her car and lost her elbow by leaving it hang out the window. I remember telling her that this was impossible without losing the whole arm. I was using my discernment even then.

She told tons of stories like that.

She believed in many things other people didn't. Anything was possible she used to say. She told me about her haunted house when I was four, and I was hooked. She was the first to introduce the occult to me.

I was always intrigued by ghost stories and the unknown, as far back as I can remember. When I was eight or so, my mom bought me a book from the Scholastic Book Fair (remember those?). In that book, there was a supposed "real photo" of a ghost on a staircase. (I guess that it became a very famous photo at one point). I stared at it for hours. I knew that it just had to be real.

I grew up listening to the stories of my grandparents, too. They were German, Pennsylvania Dutch dairy farmers. (Mennonites for some who don't know). They owned a hundred acre farm on the Sugar River about a half hour away from our town I grew up in. Both spoke German. Both were also totally superstitious. I spent a lot of time on Sunday afternoons there, after church, and at family dinner, hearing stories.

My grandma used to tell me stories about growing up and weird things that used to happen. She said that there were two brothers who could do magic, and they could go to farms and make "gold" roll from a goose's nose and then disappear. She referred to them as "witches." She actually saw this happen, she said. She was terrified, and I remember thinking that I enjoyed her reaction more than anything. Of course, most people dismissed her stories, but I listened intently. I listened to any story I could. My interest continued to grow. I looked and listened for any stories that I could find. I listened to friends and their friends. I loved to be scared, and yet, I wasn't. That should've told me something then. I was more amazed than frightened.

I didn't know that I had ability growing up. I am convinced, though, that those of us who often have strong ability are accessing prior knowledge. A follower asked recently if I thought that there was a correlation between intuitive ability and sleepwalking. I truly don't know, but I did sleepwalk for several years of my adolescence. Everything I did pointed to intuitive ability. I just didn't know it yet.

My astrological chart says in five places that I'm a psychic. This includes my Pisces moon. It also says that I am a searcher for the truth and how I perceive them. I'm a Sagittarius, and we are always interested in higher truths and spirituality.

For those of you who don't follow astrology, it's real. It has to do with time and how patterns repeat themselves. While I am not an Astrologer, I do understand Astrology somewhat and appreciate it for what it is. I use it when I do readings. It all has to do with time.

Time is such an esoteric thing; we haven't discovered even a fraction of how it all works yet. If you've never had an astrological chart done, I highly recommend it. Some of the information is not only helpful, but amazing as well. Even my mother believed in it, and she was a super "holy roller" as we used to say. Over the years, I have learned a lot of behavior and patterns. I personally ask people when doing a reading for their Sun, Moon, Rising and North Node. Sometimes I ask for their Mercury.

Remember, you need to have your birth time, birth date, and birth location to find your full chart, and as close as possible to the exact minute. For me, within one minute difference, my signs change. I am not even one degree in Capricorn. I wonder how many people there are who don't have the exact minute of birth on their birth certificates. It can actually change their astrological charts. I'm pretty sure, though, it's accurate. I'm such a Capricorn Rising, it's not even funny.

For those who don't have their time of birth on their charts, I give them this general rule. Ask your mom about what time she thought you were born. If she cannot remember, pay attention to what time you're at your best. Are you a morning, afternoon, evening, or night person? Studies have shown, like I said before, that our circadian rhythms are set at birth according to the time we are born. If you can't get the time exactly, maybe you can get within an hour or so. After a while, as you understand Astrology better, it might help also.

I am very good at picking up on what signs people are. I do not, however, know much about transits. I am still learning. Astrology is very complex, and people study for decades. These are a few things that I have noticed about astrology and their signs. This is just a brief list.

What I Know About Astrology

1. Rising or Ascendant Signs are sometimes more important than your Sun Sign. Your rising sign is how you appear to the world. I always pay close attention to this when I do readings as a side note of the person. I always pay close attention to the Ascendant Sign.

2. Your Sun is who you are at your core, the real you. I often see that some signs differ throughout the month. For example, November Sagittarians are a little different than December Sagittarians.

3. The Moon is your emotional side and how you feel about yourself and others. I think it's very difficult at times to be a water sign moon (Pisces, Cancer, Scorpio). It makes you almost overly emotional. The moon is especially important to some people more than others, I think if perhaps you've been born at night.

4. The twelve signs are broken onto four elements, **Fire** (Sagittarius, Leo, and Aries), **Air** (Aquarius, Gemini and Libra), **Water** (Pisces, Cancer and Scorpio), and **Earth** (Capricorn, Taurus and Virgo). People act like their elements. Fire often have fiery tempers and are always moving and on the go all the time. They are also the life of the party. Air signs are great communicators, well-liked and prefer to use the air to verbally communicate. They are also usually well-liked by everyone. Water signs are very soft and emotional, like tears (of sorrow or of joy). They are often caregivers. Earth signs

are grounded, logical, and steadfast. Earth signs may also love animals, nature, and gardening.

5. Your North Node is what life lesson you are working on in this life. Your South Node is what you were working on in your last life and now are mastering. More about this later. (You hit your North Node usually around thirty-seven to forty or at fifty years.) When you are truly working on why you came, things seem to be effortless, if by magic. That's how you know you are in your Life Lesson.

6. You'll never learn everything in Astrology. You can study thirty-forty years and still learn things. The intricacies blow my mind.

7. There is no real right or wrong way to do Astrology. There are types of Astrology like Vedic, Evolutionary, and Western Astrology. Some are almost philosophical in nature.

8. Astrology has to do with time and how patterns repeat themselves. I always compare it to history and how it repeats itself in cycles. I also believe that formula $E=MC2$ applies to astrology.

9. Astrology IS true and does work if you understand your own chart and how to read it.

10. Astrology is biblical. The Wise Men were Astrologers, not astronomers. Jesus has inadvertently mentioned it a few times. One place is: "There will be signs in the Sun, the Moon and the Stars." (Luke 21:25) In Psalms 19:1-2 it states "The Heavens proclaim the glory of God; the skies proclaim the work of his hands, Day after day they pour forth speech, night after night they reveal knowledge."

11. I think Astrology was created by God as a broad map based on time and patterns. Organized religion has brainwashed everyone into believing Astrology is evil because they want

control. Knowing how to look at your life and take charge and make decisions means not depending on anyone. If no one has control over you, organized religion would no longer exist. We can understood everything at a soul level. That is what is happening in the Age of Aquarius, which is right now.

12. Transits and retrogrades are real, especially Mercury-in-Retrograde—and a pain in the ass! If you don't know what that is, it's when Mercury appears to move backwards in the sky. It happens usually three-four times per year, for about three weeks. It's a time to re-evaluate and heal old relationships, to find peace and let go of other things. I know for me, I remember crap from my past that is unresolved. Someone from the past might pop in at this time, or you may have a disagreement. It's not the time to sign papers or contracts. Everything is messed up, especially electronics. Pay attention, you will notice crap. I have a shirt that says, "Hide me, it's Mercury-In-Retrograde."

13. I've found that if Mercury-In-Retrograde is in your sign, for example if it's in Sagittarius, I have either a really good Mercury-In-Retrograde, or a really bad one. There is no in-between. Yes, on occasion you can have a good one. It's not always negative.

14. Your opposite sign is usually drawn to you for some reason. The opposite of you is six signs difference. I am a Capricorn rising, and everyone in my life is Cancer—and I mean everyone; from my best friend, to my husband's best friend, to my nephew, to my grandfather. It's more than a coincidence. These people are emotional, and I offer stability. In return they give me the emotional aspects of life.

Astrology Signs: What I Know to be True about a Sun, Moon. or Rising in These Signs

I am not an expert. I will admit that. But there are certain things that I know to be true about certain signs. There is good and bad in all signs. These below are sun signs, but your moon sign and Rising (Ascendant) can also have the same attributes. Remember, Sun is who you are, Moon is how you feel, and Ascendant is how you appear. These are just a short rundown of how I see things.

Pisces

Pisces are emotional and lack self-confidence. They constantly second guess themselves. Pisces are extremely intuitive and are probably psychic or healers. They usually love animals. They are extremely empathic, and because of this, are taken advantage of by others often. Pisces need more sleep than the average person and get a lot of their psychic downloads while asleep. Downside: Pisces are often emotional messes, immature, and overly emotional.

Aries

I don't wanna say Aries are selfish, but there is a general desire to put their needs first and that is the most important. These fire signs have lots of energy and can be very bossy, with the need to be number one on their minds often. They can be very competitive. They set goals and reach them. They are good manifesters. Their motto is, "Lead, follow, or get outta the way." Downside: Aries can be egocentric, domineering, aggressive, and selfish.

Taurus

This sign is not fast moving but gets the job done. Sometimes they procrastinate but are more likely to just take their time doing things. I've seen Taureans make tons of money, lose it, and make it back again. They are great at making money. They can have a creative streak. They are dependable and logical. They are stubborn and strong-willed. They can be great gardeners. They are reasonable, practical, and sensible. They have a "never say die" attitude. They appreciate art, beauty, and the finer things in life. Downside: Taureans can be my way or the highway attitude. "I'm always right," have a big ego, or only see things in black or white. Some Taureans can be lazy.

Gemini

Geminis are very creative and very likable. Since they are air signs, they are great at communication, especially verbal and might be somehow in the public eye, guest speaking, etc. They are often lots of fun with a great sense of humor. They never take themselves too seriously. Geminis often change their lives somehow at least once, flipping everything. Geminis can be a lot of fun. Downside: Geminis are sometimes two-faced and change their minds on a dime. They can also seem like they have their head in the clouds.

Cancer

Cancers are one big ball of emotion. They don't want you to know that they are a mess inside. We all know, but they think we don't know. They try to hide it but can't hide their emotions well. They are extremely empathic. They usually love animals. They are often caregivers. Downside: They are extremely needy and can suck you dry emotionally. They can also be passive-aggressive and manipulative. They also do the "poor me" thing. They often suffer from depression.

Leo

Leos crave attention. They need to be in the limelight in some way, like giving speeches, on Social media, etc. They can have hot tempers but forgive freely. They are extremely family oriented and protective of those they love. They are loyal. Their bark is worse that their bite. Their personality is truly the epitome of the lion on the *Wizard of Oz*. Leos and Sagittarians really like each other. And get along famously.

Downside: They can be procrastinators. They say they are going to do something and truly mean to, but they get sidetracked. They also sometimes can have big egos.

Virgo

Virgos are psychic. They are grounded, practical, and organized. These people are often anal with organization. A lot of them like governmental organizations where there is structure. They are almost always good with money in some way. They are very powerful. They don't play. Do NOT piss off a Virgo! Downside: They can be controlling, manipulative, and vengeful.

Libra

Libras are likable, good communicators and search for justice for all. They are often in the beauty industry or seek out beautiful things that they think are beautiful, like art. They may even be physically attractive. They have high morals, and their ethics concentrate on the collective attitude, "Can't we all just get along?" Downside: Judgmental and think that their beliefs are the only truth. They can also be very vain.

Scorpio

Scorpio are workaholics. They are led by Pluto. Fear invades their lives. The first thing I ask a Scorpio is, "What are you afraid of?" I feel this is one of the hardest Astrological signs to be. They are always seeking transformation. They are very intuitive and emotional. They are extreme perfectionists, and their own worst critics. They thrive on drama and often create this without even knowing it. Scorpios always strive for something better and are never happy with the status quo. Downside: They often have pity parties for themselves. They often ask, "Why me?" They can be extremely vengeful and overly emotional. Don't ever cross a Scorpio!

Sagittarius

Sagittarians are outgoing, extroverted, and life of the party. They are witty and like the limelight. They love learning and higher education. They are fascinated with the human mind and how it works. They are philosophers. They wanna know, they wanna know, they wanna know. They are extremely spiritual. There are two types of Sagittarians—extremely loyal or ones who cannot stay loyal if they tried. They are extremely optimistic. They love to travel. Sagittarians also are a little bigger than most people and need heavy exercise. Downside: They can have huge egos and are often narcissistic. They are often fickle in relationships, and too Pollyanna.

Capricorn

Capricorns are structured, reliable, dependable, and steadfast. They like to make lists and mark off when accomplished. They are the business owners of the Zodiac. They respect hard work and fortitude. Their emotions are under control and use the logical side of the brain. Downside- Too rigid. Often follows the societal rules TOO closely. Not a risk taker. Can be boring.

Aquarius

Aquarians are bubbly, creative, and likable. They tend to enjoy or try to live in the moment. They LOVE technology and electronic gadgets. Most of the time, this sign doesn't care about material things or possessions. Cooperation, creativity, and love is their motto. Downside: They appear "spacy" and can have poor money skills. They are often too idealistic and get caught up in a fantasy world.

Cusps: Yes, I believe in Them.

A cusp is the belief that we are influenced by the sign before or after our birth sign. (This is in reference to your Sun sign, by-the-way). It's kinda like a "shadow period." This time frame is usually within two to three days with the cutoff of each sign.

So for instance, I am a Sagittarian cusp. The change of the sign is the 21st of December, and the cusp range is the 18th-23rd of December.

Many astrologers do not believe in cusps. They say that you either are this sign or that one. I say that cusps are real. Unless you are cusp, you probably haven't experienced it.

Cusps are almost an oxymoron. A lot of times, the signs near you are very different than your Sun sign. I am a fun loving, intellectual Sagittarian, mixed with the practical, down to Earth no nonsense Capricorn. It almost creates a dichotomy in us cuspers.

I know that while I am a Capricorn rising, I am a Capricorn cusp. That could be affecting my heavy Capricorn energy, but I've talked to many cuspers who all say the same thing. They seem to be both signs. Maybe we all want to feel special by saying we're cusps. I still believe that shadow periods like this are real. All I know is that it is very real for me. These cusps even have names, so I guess the jury is out. Here is the breakdown.

Pisces/Aries March 17-23–Cusp of Rebirth

This is considered the start of the Zodiac Year, which means A death and rebirth. I find it not unusual for these cuspers to completely change their life at some point and hit the reset button. They may even do this more than once in their lives. Downside: They let people take advantage of them.

Aries/Taurus April 16-23–Cusp of Power

This is an extremely powerful cusp with tons of "Never Say Die" Energy. They are leaders with a strong Will to succeed. Their intense energy, drive, and ambition is a sight to behold! Downside: They are extremely stubborn and must have their own way.

Taurus/Gemini May 16-23–Cusp of Energy

Yes, these people are full of vitality and are super creative. Their minds and bodies seem to move a mile a minute. This sign and cusp is interested in beauty and the finer things in life, so the intense news of that and the likability and communicative nature of Gemini creates a striking combination. Downside: They can be rigid and feel that their way is the only right way.

Gemini/Cancer June 21-24–Cusp of Magic

These people are creative and extremely sensitive. They are able to manifest well. This sign is a great combination of thought and feeling. Downside: They let their dreams and emotions get the best of themselves.

Cancer/Leo July 17-23–Cusp of Oscillation

This cusp vacillates between emotions, empathic ability, and the wish to be noticed. While Cancers can like to be in shadows at times, Leos love to stand out and like the attention. Cancers are introverted, Leos are extroverted. It's a huge juggling to balance the energy. Downside: They can procrastinate when overwhelmed and can be passive-aggressive.

Leo/Virgo August 19-25–Cusp of Exposure

This cusp is dynamic and charismatic. They have high intuitive ability. These people are vulnerable, yet grounded. They are detail oriented. They are gifted at persuasion. They are dependable and carefree at the same time. Downside: They can be controlling and manipulative.

Virgo/Libra September 19-25–Cusp of Beauty

These people truly are beautiful, inside and out. They usually have something to do with beauty and the beauty industry. They love things that are beautiful. Yet, they are grounded and practical. These people are also very intuitive. They deeply care about other people and social justice. Downside:They may be control freaks or be vain.

Libra/Scorpio October 19-25–Cusp of Drama and Criticism

These people are critical of others, but even more so with themselves. They create drama in their lives and don't even realize it.

Nothing is ever good enough. They are probably attractive. They are very intuitive and can see right through people. They are very hard workers. Downside: They complain and blame others a lot.

Scorpio/Sagittarius November 17-22–Cusp of Revolution

This cusp is a mover and shaker. It has a need for change and isn't afraid to do it. They are passionate, energetic, and have the ability to see the bigger picture. They are innovative, intelligent, and creative. They are great problem solvers. They are forever trying to transform themselves in some way and trying to release fear of the unknown. Downside: They can take on too many projects and get scattered, and get caught up in their own head with fear.

Sagittarius/Capricorn December 18-23–Cusp of Intuition

This is the cusp of psychic abilities. Believe is or not, I have another Lana Duncan, who was born ten years older exactly on the same day, December 19th. She is also psychic. These people are grounded, love to travel, and love education. They are ambitious and hardworking. Downside: These people can be very egocentric, domineering, and stubborn.

Capricorn-Aquarius January 16-22–Cusp of Mystery

This cusp is grounded but innovative, creative but grounded. These people are also ambition and hardworking. They are driven and are yet cooperative. Downside: Can vacillate from controlling to congenial.

Aquarius-Pisces February 16-22–Cusp of Sensitivity

This cusp is kind, generous and empathic. They concentrate on others and their needs. They are loving and selfless. They are always thinking about the higher good. Downside: This cusp may smother and create enabling. They may also be taken advantage of.

Man, That North Node!

When I am doing a psychic reading, I always take a look at your North Node. Like I said before, that's what you are learning in this lifetime. You are releasing Your South Node, which you learned from your previous life. South Nodes are your opposites in Astrology, which is six months apart. So a North Node of Pisces is a South Node in Virgo. You always start out in your South Node, coming into your North Node at around age thirty-seven to forty, or age fifty, from what I see.

Boy, you DEFINITELY will know when you are in your North Node! Things seem to flow, your sense of purpose becomes your focus, and things just kinda seem to flow! It's almost like things happen as if magic! You may not fully ever learn your North Node, and that's OK.

I hit mine at fifty. That's when I truly started all of my Social Media, podcasts, and what not.

Here is what I know to be true about the Nodes. I listed these with their opposites, so the signs are switched to compare both North to South nodes and visa versa.

Pisces North Node–Virgo South Node

Pisces North Nodes are learning compassion, empathy and working with the collective. You are also learning to trust yourself and stop self doubt. You are learning to have confidence in your intuition. Pisces North Nodes are learning **to** release perfectionism, the need for control, and the inability to go with the flow. You are also releasing complete independence and the inability to accept help and work with others.

Aries North Node–Libra South Node

Aries North nodes are learning to develop an authentic sense of self. It's finally about THEM personally. It's not about being selfish, rather putting up boundaries, and not being told what to do. It's about understanding their personal power and freedom. Aries North Node is releasing the need to seek approval from others and the need to be within social constraints. It encourages us to let go of relationships with others that no longer serve us.

Taurus North Node–Scorpio South Node

This is my North Node. It's literally learning how to make money spiritually, ethically, and positively with strength, creativity, and grace. It's learning how to stay practical, staying grounded without doubt, and yet learning balance without burnout. It's releasing self doubt, workaholic tendencies, and release of the "Why me?" attitude that the creation of drama can bring to themselves. They are learning to release fear.

Gemini North Node–Sagittarius South Node

This is a North Node of learning, searching, and open mindedness. You may be in the public eye in some way. You are searching for spirituality without constant meandering and generalizations. They are releasing the need to preach and always be right in a domineering way. They are releasing the need to "fix" things, including situations and people. They are also releasing the need to win at all costs.

Cancer North Node–Capricorn South Node

This North node is learning about compassion, empathy, and caring for others. They are often caregivers in some way. They are learning about security and emotional stability. They are learning about family values. They are releasing the need to be perfect, the lack of emotion, and the ambition of a career without emotional aspects and the need for status and materialism.

Leo North Node–Aquarius South Node

This North Node likes to stand out from the crowd, and accepts the attention that goes with it. They are often in the public eye. They are learning how to be confident and become leaders. They are learning to represent those who need to be defended and what is right and just. This North Node is releasing the collective and the societal pressure to conform, and all the peer pressure associated with that.

Virgo North Node–Pisces South Node

Virgo North Nodes are learning strength, self-confidence, organization, and fortitude. They are learning self-reliance, releasing the need to have approval from others, while learning to do things in complete detail. They get the "bigger picture" and complete their ideas to fruition. They are releasing the inability to get things completed, staying ungrounded and total idealism. They are also releasing the inability to set personal boundaries and to stop being selfless. They are also releasing overly emotional behaviors and lack of self confidence.

Libra North Node–Aries South Node

Libra North Node is learning how to find justice and fairness, in the collective or in society in some way. This North Node is learning communication, harmony, and verbal diplomacy. They are learning to seek balance and compromise. They are releasing the "me, me, me" ideals. They are releasing assertiveness, independence, and personal needs and wants.

Scorpio North Node–Taurus South Node

Scorpio South Nodes are learning about transformation and personal power. They are seeking rebirth. They want to understand everything about life. They are releasing the need for comfort, especially in the material world. They are releasing the resistance to change.

Sagittarius North Node–Gemini-South Node

Sagittarius North Nodes have a need for learning and travel. They seek higher spirituality and its connection to them and the world in general. They usually seek higher education in some way. They are releasing scattered energy and thinking in global ways. They are releasing the need to know all things without knowing those things intricately.

Capricorn North Node–Cancer South Node

This North Node is learning the precarious balance of work-life and family life. They are mastering the need to put their career and ambitions over the needs of their family or those they love. It's all about balance. They are releasing over emotionality, over giving to themselves, and selflessness at their own expense.

Aquarius North Node–Leo South Node

Aquarius North Nodes are concentrating on the collective, instead of individuality. They have a need to work with others, instead of just standing out in the crowd. This North Node may be involved in technology in some way, even investment like AI stocks. They work creatively but are collaborative. They are releasing the need for personal recognition and the need to stand out and be number one.

I use these aspects when I do readings all the time. I can almost ALWAYS pinpoint your North Node by listening to you talk. Remember it is not magic. It has to do with time and how things repeat themselves.

The Church isn't full of hypocrites . . .

There's always room for more.

Have you ever noticed that even devout traditional religious fanatics look at their horoscopes from time to time? I remember my mother wearing her Scorpio bracelet. She never viewed it as evil, even though she was ridiculously religious. I thought astrology was all silly then. My church had taught me that.

I was raised in a very Bible thumping, pulpit pounding, devil-chasing Evangelical home. We went to church three times per week: Wednesday, and two times on Sunday. I was baptized, confirmed, and married there.

That church was one of the first places I really got to understand religion and the hypocrisy it was. This congregation was some of the worst people I ever knew, especially the Youth group. The bullying that I experienced was unprecedented. My brother really got the brunt of the abuse. He was very short, and instead of what was supposed to be a place of acceptance, became a place of contempt.

I don't like to talk about it, but I grew up overweight and made to feel isolated and ashamed. More than once I was made fun of while attending that church. The Youth group belittled me, told me I was ugly. They mooed at me. One time, they made fun of me so badly that I hid under a porch at a youth camp. They told me they didn't like me because I was fat. It was painful. It still hurts.

My mom used to tell me that we went to church for "God," not for man. But I kept thinking, why should I put up with abuse? Doesn't God want me to be happy? God wants me to be tortured? How could an all-loving God want that for me? It's all my fault, and I deserve that?

Bullying is a funny thing. For some reason, the person being bullied is ashamed of themselves. Like it's their fault. The point of bullying is an attempt to isolate the victim. Isolate them from the rest of the group. And that is just what the bully or bullies did. Bullied victims often don't want to talk about it. They are ashamed that they are too fat, too poor, too ugly, too tall, too short, and on and on and on. No one ever realizes that almost ALL people have been bullied at one time or another in their lives. I didn't realize this myself until I was an adult. It's an unwritten rule for most people NOT to talk about it, Usually the bully never even has remorse. Matter-of-fact, many bullies never take responsibility for their actions.

It's not worth confronting your bully. I learned that the hard way. I had heard that confronting a bully would backfire, and how true that is! I reached out to an ex-classmate bully through Social Media. It was a fiasco, as he denied he ever did anything, and I ended up apologizing to HIM. Yeah, there is no real satisfaction in it. I just have my memories, and how I've tried to heal from them. It sometimes just takes time. It also depends on how much it happened, and for me, it was usually a daily occurrence. I was bullied both at church and school, but church was definitely the worst. I still can't believe the hypocrisy of those "loving" people. That is the reason that led me to turning from organized religion.

A few years ago, though, I did break down and attend a church for a while. I wasn't there long. Our pastor came to the congregation saying he was a porn addict and needed help. The church removed him and kicked out, no joke. Most organized religions just don't get the "He who is without sin, cast the first stone" thing. I was permanently done and still am.

Anyways, what was interesting was that there were some liberal ideas within that church, which really came as a shock when you think about it. Things like, "Did God create the Earth in seven days, or did he do it over millennia because what is a day to God? Does it matter?"

These things did make me think and helped me develop my religious views. Those experiences and hypocrisy are what led me on my path. I learned to love God but hate religion, especially the narrow-minded Bible thumpers. Just remember, we are a piece of God, and God is within you. You don't need organized religion to have a great relationship with God.

Yep, growing up, I was an oxymoron. I was fat, but yet, I was always extremely athletic and active, like I am today. I was on the tennis team, and an all-state softball pitcher. I actually played tennis tournaments with the USTA. But there, too, my nickname on the softball team was "heifer." The nickname came from my coach who just couldn't understand why I was such a "bitch" to him.

I have to admit though, this trauma made me empathetic to those who are down-trodden, and to those who don't "fit in." I get you. I truly do.

My earliest memory of knowing that I was different came to me when I was five. Everyone was getting ready to go for the day, and a little girl named Laurel was giving out birthday party invitations. Everyone got one. I held out my hand, and she said something that I'll always remember: "You're not getting one. You're fat."

That was the first time I realized that I was different. It's a theme that I have with me for the rest of my life. I'm an outsider. I'm different and never quite fit in. It wasn't until I got older that I realized that many of us don't fit a mold, especially with our thinking patterns, and those who have experienced what I have experienced. I can guarantee if you are reading this book, you are an outsider, too. There are many reasons why we don't quite "fit." And here we are together, searching for our place. I have come to understand another reason why I don't quite fit in.

Maybe you share this with me. I am left-handed. Left-handedness is a form of Neurodivergence. Many say left-handedness is not a neurodivergent quality; I say it is. Left-handed women make up only five percent of the world's population. I know that I just don't think or see things like most right-handed people. (I have another section about this later.) Matter-of-fact, I gravitate towards other lefties, without even knowing it. Almost all of my close friends are lefties, both male and female. Birds of a feather flock together.

I have forever been trying to fit in, and to find my "tribe." These people share my same thought pattern. It's my identity. I even have LEFTY on my license plate.

People used to think that being left-handed was bad, and many still do. In many languages, "left" is a horrible thing. The word in Latin for left is *sinistre*, which becomes the word sinister. One better than that is the word for left in French is *gauche* and translates to "awkward."

In the sixties, parents and teachers often changed children who used their left hands. No one knew how damaging changing a left-handed child was then. I'm glad my mother never changed me. I remember her being astounded when I first started to write.

"Look at that!" she used to say.

I was a lefty, like my dad, and I remember my mom giving specific instructions to the teacher to not "switch" her child. I remember the teacher handing me those "lefty" scissors that never worked right and turning my paper sideways so as to not smear my ink as I wrote. More than once the side of my hand was full of graphite from setting my hand on my paper as I wrote my list of spelling words. I was the only lefty in my class of twenty-five.

I loved being left-handed and discovered being different is OK. It has become my narrative. I guess that I wouldn't have developed my sense of self if I hadn't been bullied and hadn't been different. This is who I became. I knew that much. Maybe this led me to explore my psychic abilities at a greater level, realizing that yes, I'm different, but it's ok. I now embrace that. I am pretty sure that it was what had led me on a non-traditional religious path and to rebuke traditional religion. And by-the-way, pay attention, most psychics and mediums are left-handed or right brain dominant. Just an observation, but this is my "tribe," and I notice things like this. It's my narrative. It's where I belong.

Whenever I do a reading, I ask a few questions. I am a cold reader, but I might pose some specifics. The first thing I sometimes ask my clients when they schedule a reading with me is a simple question, especially when they are feeling "stuck" in their lives.

"So, Who ARE you?" Most people do not know how to answer. They really have to give it some thought. But believe me, your soul knows the answer. It knows everything, good and bad. You need to reconnect, reach in there, and find it.

Things changed when I was eight. My family's lives changed drastically when my working diabetic mother needed an experimental surgery to repair a broken blood vessel in her eye.

In the '70s the procedure was brand new, a treatment for something called Diabetic Retinopathy, and she went for surgery to repair it. Only the surgeon did surgery on the wrong eye, leaving her with 95% blindness.

I was young, but I remember clearly my mom looking out the window, watching what little light she could still see, fade. Why she never sued was beyond me. She said she didn't believe in it. She said that God must've had a reason. Her lack of being able to get out and do things led to her early death at fifty-five.

Now when one sense fades, another sharpens. It was not only her hearing that sharpened, but also her third eye. She got better and better at predicting things like pregnancies and illnesses. We used to joke about it, but her ability to predict Packer Games was uncanny. I'm from Wisconsin and the Packers are an institution. We couldn't bet on it though; we always lost. God arranges the inability to benefit from our talents. We are here to serve others.

That's one thing people need to remember about all of us with intuitive ability: our ability is there to help others. Even to this day, I do not read for myself. Sometimes I get an inkling here or there about myself, but I cannot see clearly for myself . . . and many people have asked why. The answer is simple: God blocks it.

Think about it for a minute. If we could see everything clearly, wouldn't we avoid the bad shit? How would we learn anything? God blocks our ability to see our own Akashic Records to complete what we need to learn.

I furthermore believe God blocks certain things from us as readers when advising others. He allows us to see things we can help change where there is free will. If something transformational is supposed to happen, intuitives cannot always see it.

For example, something like a car accident that HAD to happen could not be predicted because it was a destiny situation in their chart. So, let's say someone had an accident. They were taken to the hospital, where they met their spouse who was a medical student. It was preordained in their chart

Not everything is free will, but remember this is why psychics are never 100% accurate. It has to do with destiny and freewill. There's a lot more freewill than you think, but some things are not to be changed. Freewill keeps life interesting, right? Is it already in the Akashic Records? I believe it is. God knows which way you will go, but he lets YOU choose.

The Akashic Record is the same as the Book of Life. It contains everything, word and action, past, present, and future, right down to the shape of your fingernails. It contains your freewill decisions. That's where things get confusing. God gives you Free Will. He lets you choose and knows what you will choose. It's all in that book. Like I said, others can access it, but we cannot for ourselves.

So the next time someone says, "If you're so psychic, why don't you win the Lotto?" (Geez, I hear that a lot!) I just simply smile and say, "That's not how it works" and walk away.

It was interesting when I went to college, though. I was suddenly popular. You see, I was labeled as fat and ugly growing up, and even though I outgrew my fat stage, I was still fat to everyone at home. I think it's kinda like the idea that a prophet cannot be a prophet in his hometown. I was labeled and that was all.

I had tons of boyfriends in college. It was hard to get used to. It changed my narrative, at least for a little while. I suggest everyone to at least once in their lives, move somewhere where no one knows you. Change your narrative. My college days were the best years of my life.

I met my husband Dan at nineteen when I came home for my grandparent's 50th Anniversary, and I married him within eight months (Yeah, I was pregnant and my mom predicted that right, too). I moved to suburban Chicago and had my first daughter, Savannah. I had never held a newborn baby. I was surprised by all of these things. I absolutely had no idea what I was doing. I had no idea what was to come, I was only twenty-one and quite naive. My husband's family helped a lot (when they weren't talking behind my back). I was still oblivious to my ability, but yet knew what was being said about me somehow. I tried to ignore it and still listened to all of the ghost stories. I found it enthralling. Dan's family had lots of paranormal stories that they still tell today.

One such story was about my husband's grandma and grandpa. His grandma died suddenly of an aneurysm at only forty-eight. It was terrible to die so young and suddenly like that. My husband was close with her, so the shock of it was tragic.

The family attended the funeral and went through the grieving process until one night my husband's aunt told him she had something to confess. My husband's cousin, who was two, kept asking why grandma was on the ceiling. His aunt didn't want anyone to think she was crazy or to upset anyone, so she said nothing until now. She said he saw grandma "flying." That was the night of her death.

A couple weeks later, my husband's grandpa came over to their house for a visit. He was as pale as a ghost. The family was concerned.

"What's wrong?" my father-in-law asked.

Grandpa just sat there saying nothing for a moment. He just stared at them all.

Finally, he spoke, "I got a phone call today. It was your mother. She said to take care of the kids. Then the phone went blank."

Everyone shuttered.

I loved hearing THAT kind of story. I remember thinking: *Boy, I wished that kind of cool shit happened to me!* If I only knew! In spades, buddy, in spades.

We bought our first house in Rockford, Illinois in a horrid neighborhood when we were both twenty-three. The neighborhood was rundown, with a few neighbors actually having dirt floors (no joke!). It was small, but we kept it in good shape. This is where I finished my Bachelor's degree. I decided not to go into teaching and became an interior designer for about a year. That all changed, when I ended up becoming a Teacher's Aide for a year and discovered that, yes, I wanted to be a teacher and was actually good at it. I had wanted to do that since I was six years old, but pressures of outside forces talked me out of it. Everyone told me that I wouldn't make money and that it was a thankless job. Luckily, I quit listening.

I remember my first-grade teacher, Miss Pody. She complimented me often, and she was young and pretty. There were other teachers who really made a difference, Mrs. Clark and Mrs. Dixon. Each of them encouraged my writing abilities. I remember writing a story about 'How to Catch a Dragon." Mrs. Dixon told me that it was the funniest story she ever read. I love entertaining people; that's where my dream of writing was born. I remember writing stories and working on novels as early as nine years old.

Always pay attention to your childhood dreams. Your soul knows which way to go, and at a young age, it doesn't sidetrack you. Because you are freshly here from the otherside, you remember why you came, and what you came to do. What you wanted to be as a kid is what you should've been doing. Sometimes we outgrow some of the desires, but most of the time those desires don't go away. I wanted a pony my whole life; now I own three.

We get sidetracked by others telling us it's silly or unachievable. Listen hard to that pit of the stomach. That's where the soul sits. Those childhood desires never really go away. They are your soul speaking. Listen.

I began teaching during my second pregnancy. Matter-of-fact, I taught the day I went home and had my second daughter, Ariana. I dreamed about her before she was born. I knew she would be blond and look a lot like my mom. I gave her the middle name of my grandmother. All my kids have names related to family. It's important because the person you are named after is almost always your guide after they pass. It's a great way to build relationships from the other side.

I knew I was pregnant before the test was positive. I wanted a boy and found out maybe two hours before I had her that she was a girl. She was a holy terror from day one.

My youngest daughter was totally unplanned. I wanted one more child. She was much younger than her older sister by nine years and five years younger than the middle. To this day, I remember clear as a bell, when we brought Aislan home to Ari, she asked, "We need to put her back. I wanna be the baby." Too late, kid!

Yes, Aislan was a happy accident. I have to admit though, that when I found out on the ultrasound, it was another girl, I was totally depressed. Aislan ended up being our entertainment. She was the funniest kid ever. I wouldn't have traded her for the world.

I was finishing my Master's degree in the middle of all this when I found out I was pregnant with Aislan. I still did not believe that I didn't miscarry. I was being harassed by a hellish principal and staff.

Let me tell you: teachers and their jealousy are unparalleled. Other teachers cannot stand when students love a certain teacher over the others. They will go any length to destroy that teacher and her reputation. I had a principal who was miserable, who was getting fired at the end of the year and wanted to take people down with her. She refused to renew my contract, even though I had done nothing wrong. She threatened to walk me out early when the kids protested my firing. I frankly was TOO good at my job. The harassment was almost unbearable. Everyone hated that principal.

One evening, I was laying on my bed, totally exhausted and worried out of my wits. We had just bought a new house in Roscoe, Illinois, an upscale neighborhood so we could put the kids in the best schools. I had no idea HOW we were going to make that house payment. This was one of the first times when I heard something that I will never forget. I was trying to calm down, when I heard from my right ear,

"Calm down, everything will be alright." Immediately my whole body just relaxed. I now know for sure, that was an angel. My soul knew it.

I finished my Master's Degree eight and a half months pregnant with Aislan. And then I started another school from hell, where I walked out of. Finally, I had gained a mentor who had found me a job in the Rockford Public Schools. It was not an easy position, but I was glad, and it worked out wonderfully.

Yes, I worked full-time, had two at home, and finished my degree while pregnant. Just a typical modern superwoman. I returned to work when Aislan was only three weeks old. I had no choice at the time. I had kids to raise. Welcome to America.

I started as a Special Ed teacher in Rockford primarily as a Diagnostician. I didn't become an Art teacher until I burned out of Special Ed a few years later. I worked with kids identifying their processing issues and wrote plans for them. My ability to zone in on their problems was uncanny. I knew a lot about each kid; I also taught some, and the kids were glued to me, kinda like the Pied Piper. These kids wouldn't behave for anyone but me. I didn't realize it at the time, but I was and still am an emotional healer. One of my supervisors used to say, "I wish I could bottle what you do." I still didn't understand yet. I was using my abilities even then, just not aware of it.

The school that I taught in was an old, brick building. It was a two story, with no air conditioning, the type all of us in our generation experienced. It had been a High School and then converted to an Elementary School. I remembered hearing stories about the building. The building was rumored to be haunted. I think that school buildings are especially haunted because of all the activity, good or bad. Lots of souls, lots of good and bad. I remember one story well.

Supposedly, there had been a pool, and a young girl had drowned. Late at night, you could hear footsteps of a running child. That was eerie and yet again, intriguing. I wondered if anyone had actually seen her. I did know, however, that you could definitely sense "something" in that building. A presence perhaps? I came to realize later that I could sense presences. I thought many people could. I wasn't that unusual, I guessed.

You know, everyone has their gifts; some develop them and hone their talent. Mine I think developed both from a combination of trauma and destiny. I bet I would have been a real bitch if the bullying hadn't happened. Things that happen to us can really bring out our talents. It's all a process, good and bad.

For many people, by-the-way, they do not come into their gifts until around thirty. You can have ability before this, it just hasn't really matured yet. You just haven't had enough experience and built enough confidence yet.

I get readings from others, and I personally won't get a reading from anyone much under forty. It's not that they don't have ability at a younger age. They just haven't mastered the art of delivery yet, and as we all know, practice makes perfect. Young people just haven't mastered their symbols, verbiage, and the way needed to give messages yet. I've seen some young people who are good at counseling, so sometimes it's not the case. Just remember, in my opinion, wisdom trumps age.

Thirty is when it all happened to me. My trauma is what triggered my ability. What happened next changed the very core of my being and put me on my path.

Can a Thirty Year Old be an Orphan?

I 'll never forget that day. It was two weeks before the school year was to start. I was working in a small residential teaching facility, subbing for those on vacation. I had been extremely stressed out the school year before after being harassed by a principal (nothing new, ask anybody that has taught). I wasn't sure what was going to happen. But that day, about 8:30 a.m., as I was driving to work, I suddenly pulled over to the side of the road and threw up. I chalked it up to nerves from my stressful job.

I went about my business, and about 10:30, I was called into the office. In 1997, not many people had a cellphone yet. I picked up the phone.

"Hello?"

It was my dad. "Your mom is gone." His voice was shaky and trailed away.

"Well, where did she go?" I asked, not comprehending.

"She had a massive heart attack this morning. The paramedics took her away. She had no pulse when I checked her."

I understood why I felt so sick. I felt my mother die. The cord was cut.

We all have silver cords to people we are connected to. It even mentions it in the Bible: "Before the silver cord snaps, and the golden fountain is shattered, and the pitcher breaks at the fountain, and the wheel falls shattered into the pit." Ecclesiastes 12:6-7.

We have a silver cord connected, especially to our mothers. It has been proven that after birth, mothers keep cells of their children in their bodies. I guess this proves the psychic and silver cord connection. That's why mothers have such a close intuition with their kids. They are literally connected to their offspring.

We are connected to important people in our lives, and we are also connected by a silver cord to our bodies. We often astral travel, and our souls kinda "walk out of" our bodies. We return every night via the silver cord. Ever have that slamming or falling feeling while falling asleep? That's your soul leaving to "wander for the night." When you awaken, if your soul isn't there, it uses the silver cord to "slam" you back together in conscientiousness. That's that weird "falling" feeling that you experience. You are slamming back into your body too fast after being "gone" for a while.

You can correct this, though. Next time you go to bed, tell your soul to make a gentler exit and entrance when re-entering your body after a night of traveling. Trust me, your soul will listen. I know that I tell myself to exit through my feet. I haven't crashed back into my body for years.

You see, we leave our bodies and travel a lot. It's called Astral travel. We visit dead loved ones, and sometimes, live loved ones also. But most of the time, we are visiting the otherside. Remember, that is really our home, and we are homesick. This is also why we need sleep. We need to do our astral traveling. And the silver cord helps us keep attached so we can find our bodies, and those we are connected to in this life.

So, I felt the silver cord to my mom break. It's interesting that I threw up. The cord attaches where the soul sits, which is right above the navel. I literally felt sick in that spot at the exact time she died.

It took me a few minutes to process what my dad said. No way, he's wrong. My mom has always been sick; we had nearly lost her to cancer, and she pulled through. She just had her gallbladder removed and pulled through. She was a severe diabetic and had pulled through. This just can't be right.

My mother and I had a tumultuous relationship. I always thought she was a nag. She was extremely overprotective (due to her blindness), but it drove me crazy. As a freedom loving Sag, no one tells me what to do. She and I even had an argument a few days before her death, and I refused to talk to her. My guilt was unmeasurable.

The principal at this place I was subbing was a really good guy (whatcha know! often hard to find!) and drove me home. I wasn't sure what to do, so I went to my parent's home. One of my aunts was there. She was there to help clean up and to be there for my dad. (May I remind you that we release all of our body fluids upon death). The movies never give the actual gruesomeness of death. This is the first death of someone close I had really experienced.

This is when it all started, my supernatural life and a journey that I'm still on. My aunt Robin pulled me to the side and said something that I will never forget.

"I talked to your mother on the phone last night. She told me how much she loved your dad and said she would have never changed a thing. She also told me how she wanted her funeral if something should happen. It was like she knew. She also always prayed that she'd never see the death of her own parents. And she didn't."

I quickly realized that, yes, we know when it's time to leave. We plan our charts. We have exit points. I think back now to so many other people who have similar stories. It's definitely more than a coincidence. (There are no such things as coincidences, by-the-way. It all happens and is orchestrated from the otherside.)

That night I cried in my husband's arms. I felt lost. You don't realize how much time you spend in your life trying to win your parent's approval until they aren't there. My whole identity was now gone. No one to please but myself? That was overwhelming.

This is when it all started. Actually, my best friend Shawn was the person who got me started in all this. She had me go to a psychic a few weeks before my mother's death. I was raised in a super religious background. I was a little scared. Remember I was raised in a strict religious home. This woman was dark? Evil? I didn't know what to think. But I went to her.

I will never forget what she said.

"I see you comforting an older woman with dark hair."

"Hmmm . . .," I said, suspiciously.

"This isn't good. It seems like it might be a funeral." (Notice the lack of details? This was destiny at play. If I knew it was my mother, maybe I could've prevented it, and my own transformation would have been delayed. These episodes occur so that we are to warn that person. For me, it was our destiny for my mom to die when she did.)

I nodded. "Maybe my grandfather, who was nearly ninety. My grandma has dark hair."

I had no idea that I'd be comforting my own grandma from losing her child. The natural order of things was off. There is probably no greater pain than burying a child. My grandmother passed away within a year-and-a-half after. It was an aggressive form of Parkinson's, but I believe a broken heart.

That night of my mom's death, I will never forget. That night I woke up, to a definite imprint of someone sitting on the edge of my bed. There was no doubt. I couldn't see her, but I could feel her.

We had a conversation. She told me that she loved me and would always be around. She also showed me beautiful crystal-clear glass windows. Her sight was restored.

I kind of laughed to myself, knowing that she would have been abhorred at me getting involved with all of this "evil" psychic stuff. I have to admit, her death freed me to be the psychic medium that I am today. I now only had to answer to myself and my own beliefs. Funny thing is: she must've known the REAL truth, but she contacted me tons of times. It's my truth.

That's the funny thing about all of this and the repeated message I get a lot from those who have crossed. The first thing they often say to me is; "now I remember the truth and who I am." Their religious dogma seems to be gone, and just their real soul is there.

REMEMBER: this life, like all the others, is just a role like a movie. It's not who you really are; just like Shakespeare said, "All the world's a stage, and all the men and women merely players." Remember, you are infinite, wise, and are created as a tiny piece of God.

Recently, I had a follower call me in tears. Her husband had a heart attack and literally dropped over the sink while doing dishes. She called me to see if I could connect.

The first thing he said to me to tell her was, "Make sure you give to the poor. Especially the immigrants."

I repeated this, and she gasped.

"What's wrong?", I asked.

"He was a White Nationalist and very against immigration here."

There was silence for a moment. I then heard a regretful, almost embarrassed voice say from the other side.

"I remember who I am now. I was brainwashed."

I related this information to her.

"Thank God," was all she said.

So, we remember who we are, and we reconnect. I'm not sure about how all this works, but our souls can be in more than one place at a time. (Kinda like teleporting, I believe.) I think everyone is everything, and everything is everyone. It's all interconnected, and so are we to each other.

Knock-knock: Who's There? BOO. Who? Quit whining.

At first, I noticed weird stuff. The paranormal episodes started small, getting bigger and more noticeable. I was still not hearing but was beginning to pay attention. This is often how a spiritual awakening happens; a traumatic event starts the gears turning, and situations start occurring that cannot be explained by any other way. We all know that entities can control electronics, just like my husband's grandma left a message to his grandpa. I believe this is because they, too, are pure energy.

My first occurrences were the phonecalls. The ones that came at 5:00 p.m. every day for several months.

In 1997, we still had a telephone landline. If you don't know what that is, it means that a phone was connected to my house. Cellphones and other media weren't available yet. The fact that I need to even explain that, makes me feel old! But technology is ever-changing, I guess.

When my mom was alive, she would call nearly every day after her insulin shot. That darn phone rang for weeks at 5:00 p.m., and no one was there. I knew it was her, though. But this was MY first paranormal experience like my husband's family had received. The left side of my brain just couldn't process it correctly. So, one day, I called the phone company. They simply told me that no one had called on their end. Nothing going in or out at that time or date. Yeah, I just wanted confirmation.

A few months later, I finally did buy my first cellphone (those old, indestructible flip phones, remember?). I knew mom was around, but she thought it would be funny to start playing with it. Entities do this to be funny like I said, or just get your attention. Electronics are easy for them to manipulate, since both are pure energy. Many clients of mine have had the same experiences.

One day, my phone disappeared. I couldn't find it anywhere. To this day, I still swear that the phone was on the passenger seat of my little Ford Festiva. It was nowhere to be seen. I tore that car apart. Matter-of-fact, it disappeared for more than two days. It wasn't until nearly the end of the week, and I went out to get into my car that was inside the garage. There the cellphone laid, right on the seat where I had last seen it, still working and charged. Again, no way that could've happened without some paranormal help. Quit playing, mom.

After a while, things settled down electronically. I really didn't feel her around anymore, but I knew she was somehow there. Remember, your loved ones never leave. You just become used to the energy of their presence.

With all this happening, this is about the time that my best friend Shawn asked me to go for Reiki training. I thought it would be a good thing. I found all of this to be fascinating. She had also taken me to a class where you regress to the trauma of being born. No, I couldn't remember that, but as I went through the class, I cried my eyes out. I'm sure my soul was screaming, "Oh my God, why did you come HERE again?" It was enough to make anyone cry. This is where I was introduced to Reiki.

REIKI

For those who don't know, Reiki is one of the many types of healing arts, and the most popular. It literally is a take on the essence or meaning of "the laying of hands." It was developed in the twentieth century by Mikao Usui, the Japanese Buddhist. It has to do with the aura and the seven chakras, or energy centers of the body.

It's a premise based on the fact that we are all pure energy, and we constantly absorb and release energy from our bodies, which can be manipulated to release pain and promote healing. The energy spins like a wheel and can get blocked. Chakra in Sanskrit means "Wheel."

There are seven energy centers. Here is a quick run-down in case you didn't know.

The idea is to keep those wheels spinning, opening and closing. The other idea is to try to learn to keep all of them the same size, as a means of balance. That is what Reiki practitioners do: they help remove the negative energy and help get the flow of positive energy moving.

When you activate certain chakras, one may get bigger than the others. If you are painting for instance, your Sacral chakra, which is your creativity chakra, may be brighter and larger. The task to master is to try to keep them in balance, with no one chakra being bigger or smaller than the others. It's harder than it seems, but well-balanced chakras are a sign of good physical, mental, and spiritual well-being.

When out of balance, illnesses and emotional problems can develop. The spinning wheel may discontinue its spinning and become blocked. On the same note, chakras that are too large can have nearly the same impact. This is when negativity sets in. Trauma and even world events, good or bad, may influence the sizes of your chakras.

Each of the seven chakras are represented by colors, which are in turn often appearing on our bodies. These colors of our auras relate to some of the things we are feeling or going through at the time. Let me give you a short rundown of chakras, then auras.

7th The Crown Chakra (Sahasrara), Purple, is at the top of the head. It controls higher consciousness. This is where your ego sits. This has to do with your openness and willingness to see things through other viewpoints. This chakra is greatly affected by meditation and mindfulness. When open and in balance, it accepts others' ideas and searches for their own truth. Overactive, you let people walk on you, especially with their ideas; often taking on their ideals as your own.

If out of balance or closed, the person might be a "know-it-all" or be extremely rigid. They are usually a skeptic or cynic. They may also be a part of dogma and organized religion that only sees black or white, but poses their ideals forcefully on others. They also may like arguing or pushing people's buttons to show their power. Physical symptoms of this blocked chakra are headaches, neurological disorders, depression, fatigue, sleep disorders, or emotional issues.

6th The Third Eye Chakra (Anja), Indigo, is between your eyes. This controls your intuition and spiritual awakening. In balance, you have an inner knowing and are using it effectively. You are connected with your Higher Power and soul. You are able to make decisions, have clarity and focus. This can also be a place of creativity and wisdom. Overactive, you may have too many ideas and don't act upon them. You may also daydream way too much. Blocked, you may be judgmental and rigid. NO! is your mantra. You may also have trouble making decisions, second-guess yourself and decisions, have a creative block, or may live in a fantasy world. The blockage may manifest itself as sinus problems, headaches, and eye and ear issues.

5th The Throat Chakra (Visshudda), Turquoise, is your communication center. It's where your authenticity comes from. It is about effective communication, both speaking AND listening. It has to do with being your authentic self and your self-confidence. If overactive, you talk too much, or don't let others' speak. When blocked, you cannot speak your mind, especially with your emotions. Ever get a frog in your throat and can't talk? Your chakra is blocked. The physical manifestation can be sore throats, laryngitis, or thyroid disorders

4th The Heart Chakra (Anahata), Green, is your Emotions, including love and compassion. This is where empathy sits. It has to do with emotional balance. It also has to do with forgiveness of yourself as well as others. The Heart Chakra has to do with gratitude and healthy relationships. Overactive, you may love too much at the cost of your own well being. Lonely, depressed or angry? Your chakra is blocked. Another symptom of a blocked Heart Chakra is little to no empathy, a lack of self love, and a fear of intimacy. Jealousy and possessiveness can also be found when blocked. Physical symptoms of a blocked heart chakra are lung and heart disorders, high blood pressure, and heart disease.

3rd The Solar Plexus(Manipura), Yellow, (just above your navel) is the chakra of personal power and confidence. This chakra is the seat of the soul. It has to do with that feeling you get in the pit of your stomach. It has to do with confidence and your own personal power. It's about motivation and ambition. Overactive, you are controlling or aggressive. Blocked or underactive, you may refuse to take accountability, say you're sorry, have a fear of failure, or procrastinate. The physical symptoms of a blocked 3rd chakra are within the digestive track, including ulcers, and IBS (Irritable Bowel Syndrome).

2nd The Sacral Chakra (Svladhistthana), Orange, has to do with sexual energy and pleasure. It has to do with passion and adaptability. It also has to do with creativity. Overactive, you may be promiscuous, or have a need for overindulgence or codependency. If blocked, you might feel detached from emotions, feel guilt, or have creative blocks. You may be an addict. The physical symptoms of a blocked sacral chakra are reproductive disorders, as well as lower intestinal issues and hips.

1st The Root Chakra (Muladhara), **Red**, has to do with grounding, and security. It also has to do with your physical and financial health. Overactive, you may exhibit co-dependency or want the approval of others, such as "keeping up with the Jones." Blocked, you may be materialistic, greedy, lazy, or insecure. The psychical symptoms have to do with the feet, ankles, and spine.

These seven energy centers can be applied to all living things. Animals and plants can receive Reiki too, although their chakras are aligned a little differently depending on the animal. I recommend getting trained or receiving this energy for EVERYONE.

Reiki treatment does a lot of things. It helps realign your energy and helps you heal your emotional wounds. It also clears the negativity and allows for true balance to occur. Physical ailments often clear up. I truly feel, though, that the true benefit lies when you become a practitioner.

Becoming a practitioner to treat clients opens up your Third Eye (intuition). It kinda "revs" up your intuitive abilities. It kinda kick-starts your abilities. It makes your aware of your unique talents. And the good thing is that anyone can do it.

I had no idea that this training would open up my psychic abilities, which I really didn't know I had. I didn't realize until much later that this is a common occurrence, so I was very surprised and almost overwhelmed by my new found talents.

A good friend of mine actually does aura photography (Kirlian Photography), where you can take both a picture of your current aura and chakras by computer. It was invented supposedly by Thomas Edison (who was big time into Spiritualism). If you haven't had it done before, it's an interesting experience. Many Metaphysical stores offer it. You can not only see your present aura and its color (your aura can change from minute to minute), but also your chakra sizes and if any are blocked.

In the past, I used to read at various metaphysical stores and sometimes, John, would be there, using his aura photography machine. It was humorous to see how huge my Third Eye chakra was, compared to the other chakras when I was reading. I had activated it, so it was much larger than the rest. (Sometimes, it's necessary for certain chakras to be larger than others.)

I do want to also remind everyone that while these processes open you up psychically, remember nothing helps your intuitive development more than trauma, by a single event or even repeated, as in childhood. These experiences give you empathy, which heightens your intuition.

I wouldn't wish trauma on anyone, but it is what it is. It's a revolving circle, and at its core is love and forgiveness: love for yourself, and love for those who have persecuted you. It's always all about love.

AURAS

Aura colors are an interesting situation. It's a reflection of your emotional, spiritual, and sometimes physical attributes at that time. Generally, though, your aura is one base color. Now, the base color can change, even transforming into another color. Did you also know that your favorite color is usually the color of your aura? (I will talk about that a little later.)

I'll give you a quick list of auras and what they mean. There are many colors, and often your aura is more than one at the same time. These are the basic colors and what they mean. Remember, your aura can have more than one color, sometimes even with layers, but these below explain single colors. You aura isn't usually this all the time; it's an emotional state that comes and goes.

Red: These people are creative, passionate, strong-willed, and often a leader. Some people say that red is anger, but that would be a very deep, nearly blackish-red color. This color can represent creative change or deep intensity in emotions or ambition. Red often represents a competitive "I need to be number 1" kind of person.

Pink: Pink is gentle, nurturing, kind, and innocent. I find a lot of natural healers can have a gentle pinkish color, sometimes mixed with other colors. Pink also represents creativity and artistic endeavors. Pink also represents unconditional love.

Yellow or Gold (orangey): It's transformational. You may be having a spiritual awakening. It has to do with the soul and the Solar Plexus. It's extroverted and happy. It's also athletic, even "sunny." It's a cleansing-type of color.

Turquoise: It's about healing and communication. It represents balance. You may be a healer. It has to do with the throat chakra. It has to do with set boundaries. It's calming. Since it has both blue and green, you are probably an empathic or psychic healer.

Green: More doctors love the color green than any other color. It's the sign of health and vitality. It has to do with the Heart Chakra and healing. Reiki practitioners often have a green or turquoise aura. This color is also calming, and meditative. This color dominates being grounded and of course, nature.

Purple and Fuchsia: This is the color of mystery and spiritual awareness. It it has to do with psychic ability, the Third Eye, and general empathic ability. Dark purple can represent frustration, resentment, and obstacles, while purpley fuchsia represents, love, caring, and honesty.

Blue: The color of calmness and contentment. It has to do with the Third Eye Chakra, and things seen and unseen. It has to do with self-confidence, self-esteem, and likability. (Have you ever met someone who does NOT like blue?) It exudes honesty and authenticity, empathy and compassion.

Indigo or black: I want to say as an Art teacher of thirty years, black is not a color; it is void of color. What you usually see when you think you see black is varying shades of deep green, blue, red or purple.

You do not want a black aura. It is void of emotions and energy. When I see people who have black auras, they are often sick; their energy seems to have a "hole" in it. They are also energy vampires, "sucking" the life out of everyone around them. I don't see this often. These people can also be void of the light of God. Some people refer to these entities with this aura as "Demons." I do not believe this. I think they are lost souls who have forgotten God's love. Do these souls do evil? They can.

Indigo is a lovely color and definitely a color, unlike black. People who have Indigo auras are intuitive, and in touch with the spiritual side of themselves. These people who have an Indigo aura have a strong sense of purpose and are often visionaries. They are often also empaths.

Purple: Purple auras can be considered Indigo, or fuchsia. This color is the color of mystery and psychic ability. This color is the color of higher spirituality and empathy. It can also be playful.

The More Unusual Ones

Brown: Yes, some people have brown auras. Brown is all the colors mixed together (no, it's not gray or black). Since brown is a mixture of many colors, their aura may have an overlay or perhaps turquoise and red.

Brown is homey. It literally means that the person is "down to earth." They are likable, family oriented and are considerate of others. They are very into collaboration and working together.

Metallic or Crystal: This is a very advanced person spiritually. Some people say that metallic auras are separate from a crystal aura, but I say they are sort of the same thing. This aura has a "glistening"quality to it. These people are on a higher plane. Their vibration is much higher than many people. When I see angels, they have a crystal aura, so I guess you could say, people with crystal auras are "angelic."

Gray: Gray is an aura I do not like to see in people, much like black. Where it can be one meaning potential, it is often the color of negativity, turning from the light of God, or a "lost" sort of soul. While these entities are not inherently evil, they have great potential to do harm. They have a tendency to also "hide" in plain sight. These entities have not gone evil: yet. I find it interesting where I find many gray auras. I often find them in religious settings, such as churches.

Holy Shit! There a Lot More to Colors!

I decided to add this section about colors here instead of putting them with my explanation of your birth date and color correlation. Colors are so important to me!

Colorstrology And Color Theory: Yes, Colors and Color Theory of Your Birth Date And How They Relate to You.

I mentioned before that we are drawn to certain colors because of our auras. You can also be drawn to certain colors or use them to your advantage by your birth date.

There were scientists, starting back in the fifties who studied color. They wanted to know why we like certain colors. I explained that it's often because of our aura, but it's also our birth date. These scientists believed that your behavior was also associated with color. They studied hundreds of people and realized that color truly does affect your mood, decision making, and physical responses. Certain colors make you calm, and certain colors can even make you hungry. Red, for instance, makes us hungry, so marketers use red in fast-food signs. Health is associated with green, and so most health foods are packaged in green.

Some interesting insights also showed up in the study. According to your favorite color;

1. Healers, such as doctors, liked green more than any color.
2. Those who are part of the LGBT+ communities liked purple more than any other color.
3. Optimistic people love yellow.
4. People who like black (or really indigo) are usually guarded and mistrustful.
5. Soothing colors, like blue, are used in prisons to keep the population calm.
6. If you want a good night's sleep, paint your room blue-green.

So colors affect your behavior, your subconscious, and even your life choices! As a former art teacher, I viewed color or the lack of, as the primary essence of art. Think about it; what color are you? If you could pick a color (often it is your aura), but since auras change, what color would represent you? Some people go off of their birthstones, and others by their actual birth date color.

I'm assuming that you all know your birthstone according to your birth month. If not, it's easy to find:

January-Garnet
February-Amethyst
March-Aquamarine, Bloodstone
April-Diamond
May-Emerald
June-Pearl, Moonstone, Alexandrite
July-Ruby
August-Peridot, Spinel
September-Sapphire
October- Opal, Tourmaline
November- Topaz Citrine
December Turquoise, Zircon, Tanzanite

There is a theory out there, based on your exact birth date called Colorstology (Bernhart, Pantone, 2005). All three hundred and sixty-five days of the year have a corresponding color. You can use these colors to manifest, or just appear a certain way to people. There is a whole philosophy on this.

I've noticed that the color of your birth date often corresponds to the birthstone. For me, turquoise is my birthstone (and my favorite stone at that!), a turquoisy color is my birth date, my favorite colors are yellow and turquoise, and even my eyes are turquoise. So I guess my color that represents me most is turquoise. It's the color of a healer. It all makes sense. Find out which color pops up for you like this. Start using it around you.

I am lucky that a certain turquoise color looks good on me as a Warm Spring, so I wear it a lot (Color palettes for your skin tone and hair is a whole other book!), Sometimes certain colors don't match your skin tone. That's OK. You can use it in your home, at work, etc.

I learned all of this in High School and even today, am fascinated by this whole subject. Some people don't really believe in it. I am absolutely positive that this is not only important but can be used to your advantage. Worth a try, right?

My First Real Metaphysical Dabbling

Shawn is my best friend. We have known each other since I was twenty-three years old. We worked at a now defunct retail store. She had just moved up to Illinois to take care of family, and I bought a house and was finishing my Master's Degree. We became instant friends. Under Past-Life Regression, I saw that we were nuns together in Paris. We've had a long history.

If you ever have a person come into your life, and become instantly attached, I can guarantee that you have known each other before in another life. Same goes for someone you meet and instantly dislike. They are soulmates.

Many people use the term "soulmates" incorrectly. Many people think it's the "love of their lives" in a romantic way. Some people also may call them "twin flames." Both terms are probably used wrong.

A **soulmate** is anyone who comes into your life to balance karma or teach you a lesson. This includes lovers, friends, moms, dads, friends, or enemies. Most of the time, you have known them before because they are in your soul family. Most soul families are around 2,500 people, but some are a little bigger (I think mine is). So all these people are interacting with you, playing different parts.

You usually have karma, good or bad, with them to be worked out. We trade places a lot. If you are drawn to someone and just can't quite get over it, it's most likely a soulmate with karma attached. Just be prepared that you may have done something nasty in another life, and there is payback.

A **twin soul is** someone who you have shared many, many lifetimes together. Because of this, your vibrations may match. You may think alike, like the same things, or even do some of the same habits. You may even have been twins or siblings in other lifetimes. According to Plato, twin souls can be a myriad of people, but they can also be romantic, too.

The **twin flame** is the rare one. Most of the time, your twin flame doesn't reincarnate in this lifetime and is your spirit guide from the other side. The theory of twin flames is based on the idea that Plato talked about.

In the beginning, God created humans and split them into two beings, being both male and female. These two people constantly search for each other, hoping to reunite. This is the explanation for a marriage. Now remember, twin flames also don't have to be romantic: they can be mother/daughter, father/son, and so on. Twin flames come together to do something great for humanity or the planet. Earth is a better place because of them.

I used to believe in the concept of twin flames, but now I question it. I think this concept is erroneous in many instances primarily because many people have single-handedly made the world a better place, and twin flames are not always needed.

I also think that this term creates false hope and obsessions with people who are convinced that this certain person is their "twin flame." This can cause a huge amount of grief when things don't work out, or if there needs to be a moving on. It can create control when some one says to the other, "You are my twin flame." This theory can create abuse, because each person believes that "We are meant to be together no matter what." Many relationships are not meant to be there for a lifetime. It's not like twin flames don't exist. I believe they do. It's just extremely rare and great care needs to be taken in regards to calling one as such.

My favorite type of karmic match is a friend soulmate. They are nothing more than someone who truly loves you just as you are. Some people are lucky enough to have three or more in their charts. Some have only one, and some even marry their friend soulmate. Many times, these people will not remain in your life forever, but drift in and out. They are there to bring joy and love. They are a blessing from God.

My friend Shawn was like that for me. She was always there for me. We decided to go through Reiki training together. I have to admit, she is the one who started me on my journey in a way. She showed me alternative ways of thinking.

Shawn and I went through the process, Level 1 and 2 of Reiki certification. We could've chosen other things, Quantum healing or Shamanism, but decided to go into Reiki because it was easy to find a teacher.

We learned our techniques, symbols and such, and after a couple hours, we took a break. We were asked to practice on a willing fellow practitioner. Shawn stood at one end and I stood at the other of the table with the client between us lying on a table. Placing my hands above her slightly, I started asking questions about her life. I told her what she did for a living, where she worked, how many kids this woman had. I didn't know where it came from, but I could see the "movie" in my head. Then I asked if she knew a short, gray-haired lady named Pat. I could see her in my head, smiling.

"Yes! That's my grandma!"

I saw a heart, actually several hearts in my head.

"She sends love," I commented.

Shawn smiled and whispered. "Oh my God! You're a medium!"

What do You call a funny Medium?

A COMEDIUM

I was a little surprised. Yeah, I guess I was a medium. I probably always was. More than once I had run into people at stores and knew their stories and the people around them. I shrugged it off at the time. Neat parlor trick but an extra talent? I thought about my mom again. She could see people. She had predicted a plane crash at O'Hare in Chicago that killed hundreds in the '70s. I remembered that suddenly. So, is it genetic? I asked myself.

I truly think mediumship is a talent like anything else. I'm also an artist and inherited that talent from my dad (and the fact that I'm a lefty), so it would make sense that I would inherit this talent from my mom, too.

Now there are a couple trains of thought about mediumship. Some people say that anyone can do mediumship . . . they just have to let go of fears and grow spiritually. I disagree. Not everyone can do mediumship, and some are better than others. I know tons of people who, even as hard as they try, cannot do this. They cannot communicate verbally or visually. It's a little different. Don't beat yourself up because you aren't a typical medium: ask for signs and look for answers. That, everyone can do.

Everyone has some type of psychic ability. These can be developed like mediumship.

Here are some examples that you might have.

Empath: The ability to feel how others feel. You might also absorb energy from others. You are extremely caring and always want to help others. This is a talent about love and compassion.

Healer: The ability to be an emotional, physical, or spiritual healer. You may literally be able to heal, using your intuition to diagnose or physically heal ailments. You may also be an emotional/spiritual healer where you are calming or able to correct negative energy in others.

Discernment: The ability to see clearly when someone is up to no good or have ulterior motives. This is one of the gifts of the Bible. You have a great sense of positive and negative energy.

Remote Viewer: The ability to see people, places, and situations without actually being there. You use your mind's eye to gather information.

Psychometry: Ability to pick up energy from objects and gain information around them; you can use your other talents, such as Clairvoyance to get information.

Precognition: The ability to predict future events, often through dreams, visions, or feelings.

Dream Interpretation: The ability to give messages to the dreamer through understanding the symbols and meanings.

Telepathy: The ability to read another's mind and thoughts. This is where the intuitive modalities come in. Some of them are referred to as 'Claires." Claire in French means clear.

As you begin developing your talents, you will have different modalities. These are a few:

1. **Clairvoyance:** People can see visions, people, situations, locations or even objects in their mind's eye or on the physical plane. These people can see past, present, and future events pertaining to these things. The person may also use symbolism to interpret messages

2. **Clairaudience:** These people can hear voices, sounds, music, and other things from the otherside. They can not only hear but also communicate with entities.

3. **Claircognizance:** These people just have a "knowing." They get these "feelings," often in the pit of their stomachs and are usually right.

4. **Clairsentience:** The ability to feel what others feel, or "know" how others are feeling at a given moment. It's similar to an empath, but this ability allows them to sum up situations.

5. **Clairgustance:** The ability to taste, often through mediumship. Kinda like I do when I am reading and ask someone if their grandma made great oatmeal cookies.

6. **Clairalience:** The ability to smell, like smelling cigarette smoke after talking about someone who used to smoke.

7. **Aura Reading**: The ability to read or feel auras and use the ability to help others.

8. **Channeling**: The ability to get information from Source albeit through guides or mediumship.

9. **Mediumship**: The ability to hear, see, or feel those who have crossed over and communicate with them in some way to relate messages.

10. **Divination**: The ability to use tools or messages to communicate to those who are on this plane and to give messages. There can be many ways to get information, including, Tarot cards, browsing rods, and hundreds of other tools.

11. **Automatic Writing:** This is the ability to use your body as a physical conduit to write down information as it come through from the otherside.

12. **Akashic Records Reader:** The ability to see your "Book of Life" and determine where things have initiated from, like a fear from a past-life, or repeated patterns, etc. It also tells you what you will be doing in the future. Every thought, past,

present, and future is there. Reading these often helps people release trauma and get out of "stuck" patterns.

13. **Astrologer**: I put this on here because I truly feel it's a talent. Anyone can learn Astrology, but it's their ability to put together everything, plus using their intuition. It takes talent to piece through the information and give it in a useful manner.

14. **Teacher:** I'm not sure why so many people do not think this, but teaching is a talent. Spiritual Teachers have the ability to present things in such a way that people understand concepts clearly and easily, and have patience for those who struggle.

15. **Psychokinesis**: This is the ability to move or affect objects. This is a broad term and can also affect objects or weather. I thought this was rare until I took a class and watched everyone in the class bend spoons! Every single person, even skeptics. It's literally mind over matter. Damn, our minds are powerful. We usually have more than one of these talents.

I have several of these talents, but clairaudience and mediumship are the strongest. By-the-way, your learning style affects your modality. I learn best through auditory methods. Most people are visual, auditory, or kinesthetic. I learn best that way, so it makes sense that's how I get my information. Some days are clearer than others, while other days, I get mostly visual images. I also sometimes get smells and tastes.

As an evidential medium, sometimes spirits will give me information, like how they died n physical ways. That's when I will feel tightness in my chest or a pain in my head. This relates to how they died. They are giving me information. I notice that the spirits usually give me information that I could not possibly know. This is called Evidential Mediumship. They are giving me evidence that I am talking to the right person. It's information that I cannot make up. There's no way I'd know it. Everything from silly family jokes to nicknames, I'll usually get it. It's funny, though. I seem to hear better when it is raining or snowing, maybe because water conducts electricity in the air, and these spirits are one hundred percent energy. I'm not sure. I do know it's just that some days are clearer than others.

When they (the spirits) begin talking, they give me just a word or two to start. Sometimes they say their full name. I sometimes miss their first name but get their middle name. After a few minutes, things seem to adjust. When talking to me, they give me three different scenarios so you know who they are. They may give me their full name, a relative's name, or where the entity is from. The person receiving the reading has to figure it out. I had a spirit come through one time, and I kept asking, 'Who is Rick?' I later found out they were from Puerto Rico. Yep, it happens a lot.

Everyone is different. When I teach classes about mediumship, I tell everyone that mediumship is a personal journey. You get better over time, just like any other talent. Don't push it. Let it evolve. After a while, you will see patterns and get better and better at it.

Maybe mediumship is NOT you talent. That's OK. You may be great at other things. Focus on what you CAN do. That's what the Age of Aquarius is about.

When Guides Roll Their Third Eye at Us

Here is where I'd like to mention guides. I have mentioned them a little but would like to clarify what I have learned about them. Guides communicate in many ways, often in funny or unexpected ways. My guides sometimes make me laugh or see things in a different way. I guess we need a sense of humor in this mess we call planet Earth. You have several of them and they change often throughout your life. Mine have changed several times, as you will find out.

There are seven different types of guides. Sometimes, you can have more than one type, like a spirit guide. There are seven types, maybe more, but I found these ones are the most significant. These are the ones that I find in my mediumship when I do readings. These are the ones talking to me, giving me information.

Spirit guide: Your spirit guide is a spirit that was assigned to you at birth. It is someone who has been alive, who understands the human condition. I compare them to the voice of your conscience. These spirit guides may also be your twin flame, guiding you on what you need to learn in this life so the two of you can ascend together back to the Godhead. That is the purpose of why we are truly here: to become God-like as possible. Your guides can also change throughout your life, and there can also be more than one at the same time. I have switched from my first guide, Angela, to Dances in the Wind, to now a guide who I call Red Cloud. I sometimes see Red Cloud and Dances together. I didn't see Angela, but she did return later.. These guides come in and change as you change spiritually. I also have about three or four more lesser guides that "pop" in occasionally. One is name Joe. He's a pot-smoking hippy who reminds me how to relax and take things in stride. (No, they can't smoke on the other side but go through the motions of it. Bodies don't exist to be able to ingest things.) I also have a few guides that help me read. I think it all depends on your life path and its difficulty.

Totem Animal: A Totem Animal that stays with you your whole life. It's the real you, in animal form. It represents who you are. It guides with wisdom and reflection. For me, it's without a doubt a horse. It represents strength, freedom, and tenacity. You Totem animal should represent everything you are striving for in this life.

How do you know what your Totem Animal is? What are you drawn to? What seems to be your favorite animal? What animal pops up repeatedly throughout your life? A good book is *Animal Speak* (Andrew's, Llewelyn, 2002).

Spirit Animal: A spirit animal is different than a Totem Animal is one major way. Spirit animals change often throughout your life. For example, you are seeking abundance in your life, suddenly you might be seeing buffalo everywhere. A Spirit Animal is trying to send you a message about what is going on right now in your life. Pay attention, and if you don't know what a certain animal means, look it up. You will be surprised that certain Spirit Animals will coincide with a message or a period in your life.

Fantasy Creature: I used to not believe in fairies, dwarves, or dragons. But now I know they are real. If anyone has watched any of my videos, you can literally see things flying around me. They especially appear when I have a lot of greenery around me, like my plants that I bring inside for the winter. These beings are everywhere, and one day, I taped over an hour and a half of them.

Another one I see a lot of are wood nymphs or sprites. They aren't that hard to see. These beings live in trees. Stare at a tree at night and wait a bit. I swear you will see twinkling green lights.

I have a friend who did a reading for me, and she said that "You have a lot of fairy energy around you." She had no idea of what I was seeing, so this verified things for me.

By the way, I believe that these are tulpas. A tulpa is something that exists because we believe in it. Human minds are so strong, we create things. This includes many fantasy creatures. It may include Big Foot, but the jury is still out for me. I've talked to many Big Foot hunters, and I'm starting to think that they truly are another species of human with the ability and uncanny sense to be able to hide themselves.

Any animal or creature can be one. I have a friend who swears the Big Foot is her guide, and I don't doubt her.

Ancestral or Friend: Your family comes through for me often when I am doing a reading. It may be someone that loves and cares for you. Recently, I've noticed a lot more great grandparents coming through, especially after COVID. I believe this is because a lot of our great grandparents went through the Spanish Flue Epidemic.

I often hear, "I didn't know him/her. They died before I was born." Yes, you do know them. You were with them in heaven, waiting to come to Earth.

I've noticed that if you share the same name as your Ancestral guide, like I said before, they will be your spirit guide almost automatically.

Deities

These are gods, goddesses like Thor, Vishnu, Zeus, or even Mother Nature.

Angels and Their Purpose

We are given an angel to guide us from birth. Angels have been created solely to help humans. This angel may be a lot like you and may even look like you. My angel's name is Thomas. When I was going through Reiki, he came through. I could feel his hands on my shoulders. They are here to protect you, so you can complete your mission and lessons on Earth. Angels look nothing like what we have been told. Don't be scared if you see things that have many eyes, wings, and look like a monster. That's probably your angel.

Breakdown of Angels

This all gets so confusing! Angels were created specifically to serve humans and their plight. Although we do not interact with all of the hierarchies, they are there to serve us and help humanity. Some Hierarchies only interact and glorify God, also. There are three main hierarchies of angels. This is how I understand them. There are different systems, This is the Christian Hierarchy.

HIERARCHY #1

Seraphim: These are the angels closest to God, the ones that sing his praises. Sometimes, when I communicate with others on the otherside, I can sometimes hear a low singing of hymns. I believe these are seraphims. Supposedly they have six wings. Humans do not usually see them. Only in rare cases.

Cherubim: I always think of the artwork of Raphael when I think of these "cherubs." Biblically, they look nothing like this depiction. These angels are the angels of knowledge. They are the guardians of sacredness. According to The Book Ezekiel, Cherubs have the face of an Eagle, Ox, Human and Lion. (Notice some Tarot cards, like the Wheel of Fortune, have those in the corners.) They do not interact much if any with humans.

Thrones: Act in accordance with God's will and Divine justice. I don't think it's about personal justice, but mankind. These angels do not really interact with humans. I kinda like to think of them as the executors of karma.

HIERARCHY #2

Dominions: These angels are the ones who monitor the lower angels, mostly archangels and angels. They take their orders from the higher, Level 1 angels.

Virtues: These are the angels who give people courage, who help with humanitarian issues and all things to do with nature. This is where we hear about the virtues of faith, hope, and charity. These don't interact with people so much as humanity and its betterment. They can act to bring miracles about, increase spirituality or encouragement.

Powers: These angels help combat evil. They also regulate the lesser angels. These angels protect natural and divine order. They rarely interact with humans

HIERARCHY #3

Principalities: These angels act as guides over leaders and governments. They are responsible for keeping humans out of wars, misery, and abuse. These angels help inspire resolutions to conflicts and public welfare. They act on a grand scale, helping world matters.

Archangels: These angels interact with humans. You can call on them when needed. They will respond. If you watch my social media, you will see many flying around me, especially after I have summoned them for help. They are very small and whitish-see through. They also convey messages. Archangels are the big guys. I see these angels more often than your personal angels. They have been uniquely created for the help of humans or humanity in some way. The archangels are the ones that, for me, have really helped. You can ask for anything, and you will be amazed! I surely was! I notice when I have been summoning them, they appear as numbers and actual sightings on my videos. Yes, they have little wings, and you can see them!

Angels: These are your own personal guardian angel that follows through you in your life. They pull you out of "sticky" situations and act as your conscience. Remember the old adage: "Never fly faster than your angels can fly."

Let me give you a quick rundown on the Archangels. There are sixteen to eighteen Archangels (some say more), and each zodiac has its own Archangel. Many of their duties also overlap. Angels are neither male or female. I wrote them as male or female to make things simpler. Sometimes, there is more than one angel associated with things, i.e., days of the week; etc.

Here's a short rundown of some of the more important archangels. Their colors, crystal, duties, and zodiac sign associated with them are included.

Michael: He's the big guy. He's the head of all Archangels. He carries a sword and is ready to go to battle for you. He can be asked for pretty much any help. Ask him when you need a positive outcome. He is associated with royal blue, his crystal is blue cyan, and his number when he communicates with you is 111.

Raphael: He's my favorite. He's the Angel of healing and insomnia. Invoke him to help doctors or medical professionals. Invoke him when medicines are used to speed healing. Can't sleep? Invoke him. I swear it works. I wear a medallion with his name on it. His color association is green, his crystal emerald, and his number is 444.

Gabriel: He's the Archangel of messages. He blows a horn. He brings messages and helps with communication between people. He brings revelations. His color association is white, or silvery. He is the Archangel of the zodiac sign of Cancer. His crystals are citrine or Aquamarine. He communicates through the number 555.

Uriel: Giver of wisdom and healer of trauma, enhances creativity, prosperity, intuition, and tranquility. He is associated with the Earth. He shines God's truth into the void of confusion. His colors are earth tone and black. He is associated with the zodiac sign of Aquarius, and his stone is sunstone. He is associated with the number 4.

Haniel (Anniel): Thought of as female (although angels are neither male of female) but has to do with feminine energy and the ability to copy other talents of other angels. She is the angel of intuition and reminds you to pay attention to you intuitive gifts. Call on her when you need simplicity or balance in your life. She is associated with the color pink or light purple. Her crystal is amethyst, and she communicates through the number 222.

Raziel: The Archangel of great ideas, the giver of wisdom and higher truths, protector of Heaven's secrets, esoteric information and inner guidance. He is especially helpful to energy healers and those seeking psychic knowledge. His color association is all the colors of the rainbow. Watch for the number 23 when seeking him.

Sandalphon: The Archangel of music, this angel helps you communicate through music. He is the twin of Metatron. He ascended to heaven after being an actual human (some think he is Enoch). Some say he even has wheels. His color is turquoise and his stone is turquoise and smoky quartz. When communicating, pay attention to the numbers 0 and 9.

Metatron: Archangel of God's written Word, writer of the Book of Life (Akashic Records). He is considered a guide to humanity. Metatron's Cube is a part of sacred geometry and represents how all of life is connected. His colors are represented by the 7 colors of the rainbow moonstone. He is associated with the zodiac sign Virgo.

Ariel: This angel gets mixed with Uriel but are separate. Ariel helps with healing, especially animals and plants. Works often with Raphael. Ariel's zodiac connection is with Aries. This archangel's crystal is rose quartz and communicates through number 4.

Jophiel: The Archangel who drove out Adam and Eve from the Garden of Eden. Also referred to as Zophiel, he brandished a flaming sword and seeks truth. He is the Archangel of beauty and thinking out of the box. Call on him when you are depressed or need a creative unique perspective. His color is yellow, his crystal is citrine, and the number of communication is 333.

Chamuel: This is the Archangel of relationships and what they hold, in means of unconditional love, forgiveness, equality or romantic love. Seek him when you are seeking self-love and self-forgiveness. The color associated with him is pink or dark red, the crystal is rose quartz or ruby, and the number affiliation is 7.

Zarachiel: The Angel that leads those to judgment. He is also the archangel of memory and lost objects, and the emotional healer of children. His color is purple, his crystal is amethyst, and is associated with the number 9.

Barachiel: This archangel is the carrier of prayers to God. He is also the archangel of blessings, abundance, light, and thunder. Call on him when wanting blessings, especially for others. His color is rose, rose quart is the stone, and his number 496,000 (number of active guardian angels)

Zadkiel: Angel of mercy, healing, and freedom. He helps remove negative karma and past traumatic memories. Call on him to help release negative karma. He helps people to forgive others. His number is 4, his stone is amethyst and his color is purple.

Raguel: Raguel is the Archangel of justice and harmony. He keeps evildoers in check. He is the leader of a group of angels called principalities. His number is 6, his color is soft blue, representing the cooling down of arguments, and his crystal is aquamarine. Call on him when something unjust has been done to you.

Azrael: Azrael is the Archangel of Death. He helps people pass over smoothly. He often wears a Scuthe, but more benevolent than the Grim Reaper. His color is blue, his crystal is sapphire, and his number is 666. He is not the devil or fallen angel, but acts as a go between. Call on his help for loved ones to help them cross smoothly.

Jeremiel (sometimes called Remiel): This archangel is associated as one of heaven's gatekeepers. She is known as the archangel of visions and dreams. She is associated with the zodiac sign of Scorpio. Her color is purple, and her stone is amethyst. There is no certain number for her. Call on her to help understand and process dreams.

Yahudael: Yahudael (sometimes spelled with J) is the archangel of power, strength, and oversees work. His color is dark purple or a metallic bronze. There is no real number for him. Seek his assistance when fortitude is needed. His stone is amethyst.

Sachiel(Evangeline): Sachiel is the Archangel of wealth and abundance. He helps you discover your highest purpose by guiding you through positivity and prosperity. Seek him when you are looking for prosperity or abundance, which includes the earth and all it has to offer His color is green and gold, and sometimes blue. He is associated with several days, but mostly Thursday. There is no number associated with him. His stone is sapphire or Lapiz Lazuli.

You can access your own Archangels according to your birthdate. These are the Archangels and their astrological signs. Some signs have more than one archangel.

Capricorn: Azrael
Aquarius: Uriel
Pisces: Brachiel
Aries: Ariel
Taurus: Chamuel
Gemini; Zadkiel
Cancer: Gabriel
Leo: Raziel
Libra: Jophiel
Virgo: Metatron
Scorpio: Jeremiel:
Sagittarius: Raguel

These are the Archangels and the days of the week. Call upon them on these days.:

Sunday: Michael
Monday: Gabriel
Tuesday: Uriel
Wednesday; Raphael
Thursday: Sachiel
Friday; Haniel
Saturday: Zadkiel

These numbers often appear when working with these Angels. Pay attention! The angels are trying to communicate! Something numbers also have more than one angel. Some angels are associated with more than one number.

> 1 or 111: Gabriel, Zadkiel
> 2 or 222: Raphael or Haniel
> 3 or 333: Uriel
> 4 or 444: Chamuel and Jophiel
> 5 or 555: Metatron
> 6 or 666: Haniel
> 7 or 777: Gabriel, Raziel and Sandalphon
> 8 or 888: Michael
> 9 or 999: Raphael

Working With Angels

When working with angels, I meditate and see what color comes through. Then I know who is trying to help. The messages become loud and clear this way for me. Maybe you hear things. Maybe you even feel them. Just pay attention. I can guarantee they will communicate.

A Workable Summoning to Archangels

I do not pray necessarily to angels. I pray to God, and let the angels hear it. This way they can offer their help and service. They were created for this; let them serve their true purpose!

Dear Archangel_____

I am praying for _____, and I need your help to reach my goals. Please give me what I need to be fully in my purpose and to do for the greatest good for humanity and the Earth to glorify God.

Amen

Notice this is an unselfish prayer? It is not wishing anyone harm. It is not me, me, me. You will discover, if you have not yet done so, that whenever you do something without being self-centered, you **Will** be successful. I learned that long ago. So try this, it works.

So Who Do I Think I am Asking For Money?

S o I began my journey, after learning Reiki, doing readings at festivals and on holidays. I did this for free for several years. I really had a hard time taking money. What it was is that I still lacked confidence. It was one of my friends who pointed something out.

"You know, you need to start charging money."

"Why?" I asked.

"Because you cannot keep doing things for free. It is an imbalance of energy. You can't keep giving and giving and giving. You will burn out. Money is energy. If these people cannot give you anything back, then they need to be charged. There should be no karmic debt."

She was right. I thought for a long time and decided how much my time was worth. That's how I came up with my prices. I have always refused to be outrageous in price, but I do actually feed animals and do other things with what I charge. It would be great if we could get away without needing money in this life , but that's one of the bad catches in this life. We need money.

That's one of the first things spirits forget when we return home. I talk to many crossed-over individuals who forget quickly that we need money or physical attributes like food to survive. The spirits are so happy and content on the other side that they don't need anything physical that they forget the struggle on this physical plane. They sometimes will make comments like, "Why don't you just quit that job if you hate it so much?" They forget there are complications and fear. That concept is simply gone when on the other side.. Money is truly the root of all kinds of evil, but we need it in some form and spirits forget this. It's a forgettable memory.

Don't do everything for free. It will leave you drained and resentful. Think of charging some money as refueling your tank and balancing out energy. Think about what it takes to pay bills. Don't go overboard. It is wrong to take money from those who can't afford it. I still do a lot for free to those who need it. It's all about balance. Remember exchanging services is a good way to balance energy, too. You don't always have to literally take money. Bartering is one of the best ways, and it aligns with the Age of Aquarius

Instead, ask the person what they have to offer. There are many people who I exchange services with, and no money is exchanged. Before I started charging, though, I decided to learn how to read Tarot Cards. I practiced this for several years on my own.

WARNING ABOUT FALSE OR SCAMMING READERS

I'd like to mention that one needs to be cautious about giving some people money. There are TONS of scammers out there, giving my field a bad name. You need to be very careful who you trust. It's good to figure out things for yourself or word-of-mouth from someone you know well. Some things to ask yourself.

1. Does this person have a good reputation? Have you found out any negatives about them? How do you feel in your gut about their energy? Do they make you uncomfortable?
2. How much are they charging? Can you comfortably afford it without breaking the bank? Never spend more than you are willing to give up. Do they offer bartering?
3. How long have they been practicing? Are they amateurs or professionals? Do they have credentials?

When to Run

Run, and I mean run when you come across some of these situations!

1. The reader tells you are cursed and will remove the curse for you for money. This is a scam! CURSES ONLY WORK IF YOU THINK THEY WORK! If you need familial trauma removed, look and talk to many people. Find a person that is reasonable for your budget. Say no if they try to keep charging you.

2. The Reader wants to bring back your true love for money. This doesn't really work, and if it does, there is so much negativity to that, you are in a world of karmic hurt. Trying to force something that is against free will is wrong and creates negative karma.

3. The reader wants to cast a spell bringing harm or destruction to someone else. This is a definite karmic no-no. Live and let live.

4. Any psychic or reader who thinks they know everything and can solve all of your problems. These people also will not refer you to other counselors. They may be cult-like narcissists.

I recently had a woman call me in tears. A psychic was manipulating her to believe that her bad luck was caused by a generational curse and for only seven thousand dollars this psychic would remove it.

"Just trust me!," she told my client. "We'll do this together!" RUN! RUN! RUN!

How these people pull you in is that they are con-artists who gain your trust. REMEMBER, do not spend more money than you can comfortably afford anyways. This poor client was not even paying bills, crying to me that she was cursed and couldn't pay her bills. She couldn't pay her bills BECAUSE SHE WAS SCAMMED.

Being Careful As A Reader

I have learned to be careful as a reader. I have run into several people who are energy vampires. These people want you to fix them without putting in the work. They will show up sometimes (or call) and begin making demands of me, demanding me to drop what I'm doing to listen to their problems without an appointment. These people can get very pushy. It's called boundaries, and I've been forced to block people. I deserve respect.

Then there are the ones looking to become friends with me for free readings. Since I'm not psychic for myself, I sometimes get taken advantage of in the friendship department. I've been more aware lately, though.

The last group of people are the naysayers who wanna "check me out" to see if I'm real. They make appointments, refuse to ask questions, and usually close themselves off so I can't read them (Yes, people can do that). Everything I say is wrong, even though it's correct. Another obnoxious thing they do is tell me their "loved one had a code word." What's the code word, they ask? Well, sometimes it comes through and sometimes it doesn't. I'm here to help. I am not a dog and pony show. Move along and find someone else.

There are a lot of great people, but as in all professions, there are immoral people. But reading is a two-way street. My talent is here to serve you. I will tell everyone this now, there needs to always be respect from both parties.

My Tarot Journey: Tools that I use

I pretty much bought a book and taught myself the ins and outs of Tarot cards. I had some hangups at first. I was always told they were evil and linked to the devil. I learned and perfected my knowledge, studied, and watched how things transpired.

These are a few things that I've learned about Tarot cards.

1. They aren't magic. They are mostly psychological. Anything you've been thinking about will appear in the cards. They are merely a reflection.
2. They are simply a tool. Over the years, I no longer need this tool much, since I'm a medium, that's MY tool.
3. My cards have MY energy, and I don't share my cards with anyone. Some people like to open new decks from time-to-time, but I personally don't like that. My decks are over thirty years old and are deeply connected to me. Old traditions used to say to wrap them in silk and put them under your pillow to absorb your unique energy on them.
4. Cards have general meanings, but certain cards have certain meanings that are unique to the individual. I have one card that means thirty days. People have actually argued with me, but I prove them wrong every time.
5. I use reversals, but some people don't. Reversals have their own meanings and not necessarily the opposite of the upright. Reversals have a definite emotional quality to them. It's up to you if you read reversals.
6. Numerology and astrology, it's all there. Even color matters. These cards are so intricate that they blow my mind. I use the Rider-Waite. That's the deck everything is based off of (except the deck of fifty-two playing cards. That's a whole other story). You can tell time, see numbers, everything is there.
7. You can read a deck of standard fifty-two playing cards or Oracle cards. They are as intricate as you want them to be. The reader uses more than just cards. They get messages from situations involving the cards. Learn them well.

Like I said, I connect to family and crossed loved ones, so I get my info that way. But occasionally I'll pull a card or two or may even use runes or a pendulum. There are so many things to use as tools that they are overwhelming.

These are some of the tools for divination that I've learned to read with. But just remember, I don't need the tools. I just found it interesting and can access them.

Here are just few that I know how to do. There are thousands of tools to use. I did not include all the meanings of Tarot here because it would be a whole separate book! I also use reversals, so that would be 156 different meanings, and then the spreads! I'm sure at some point I'll write a book about what I know.

Runes are about as ancient as they come. They've been around forever, and I have learned them. Runes are generally Nordic, and they criss-cross with the Tarot. Many runes symbols appear on Tarot cards. They are a good divination tool, but I still like my Tarot because there is more detail. But they are very similar.

These are what the Runes mean and what I've learned from Runes. These are just my observations:

Algiz (protection)–prosperity and abundance, divine intervention, resilience. Keeping emotions under control.

Algiz Reversed–A warning or a sense of helplessness, Someone might be trying to harm you, death, end, war or argument.

Ansuz (Odin)–messages, verbal, written, or intuitive, truthful messages that bring enlightenment. A very positive rune.

Ansuz (Odin) Reversed–Be careful who you communicate with. Things aren't as clear you need them. They don't make sense. Also can suggest laziness, biasedness, or even delusional.

Berkana (birth)–mother/child, nurturing, protection, support, creation

Berkana Reversed–Family issues, worry about family member, arguments, words said out of anger, stagnation

Blank–This rune is blank! It means, whatever you want it to, blankness, unknown

Dagaz (dawn)–Enlightenment, Transformation, new start, awakening, darkest before the dawn.

Dagaz Reversed–This cannot be reversed, very positive rune.

Ehwaz (Horse)–progress, movement, teamwork, time for change

Ehwaz Reversed–Restlessness, and dissatisfaction, time for change has not yet started.

Eiwaz (death)–Rebirth, magic, trust, harmony, journey in important things.

Eiwaz Reversed–This is a non-reversal rune.

Fehu (Frey)–wealth, prosperity, new beginnings, maintaining a balance, all about abundance and wealth.

Fehu Reversed–Blockage, financial frustration, lack, poverty, infertility. Your hard work is not paying-off. Burnout, lack of self-confidence or greed.

Gebo (gift)–Blessings from Source or an even exchange, balance, giving and getting Karma

Gebo Reversed–There is no reversal.

Hagalaz (Air)–transformation, chaos, change, sudden disruption.

Hagalaz Reversed–There is no reversal.

Inguz (Fertility)–Growth, nature, awareness, giving birth.

Inguz–No Reversals.

Isa(ice)–stillness, focus, self-control, spiritual growth.

Isa Reversed–There is no reversal.

Jera (earth or year)–cycles, manifestation, long-term plans, passage of time

Jera Reversed–There is no reversal.

Kaunaz (fire)–knowledge, creativity, process of learning, discovery, positivity, improved health or spiritual enlightenment, courage, success.

Kaunaz Reversed–blockage in understanding, shutdown, resistance, lack of direction, loss of path

Laguz (water)–imagination, 1 of wands, intuition, ideas, time of healing,

Laguz Reversed–confusion, despair, conflict, lack of understanding, take without giving, avoidance, misjudgment.

Mannaz (man)–divine, union, manifestation, relationships, community, living in balance with family or community through strength, social order, how you relate to others.

Mannaz Reversed–problems, dissatisfaction from within, you may be facing challenges from relationships, Focusing on your healing.

Naudhiz (necessity)–needs, distress, basics, sacrifice, be patient, karmic debt

Naudhiz Reversed–you are following the wrong path, unfulfilled desires, something is missing, dissatisfaction.

Othilia (Ancestral)–ancestral inheritances, home turf, like father, like son

Othilia Reversed–Loss of home, Bad karma, prejudices, inability to find joy in family ties, or loss of stability.

Peorth (Hearth)–luck, fate, renewal, unknown,

Peorth Reversed–unpleasant surprises, collapse, obstacles, failure, stagnation, loneliness.

Raido (Wheel)–ride, journey, change, new beginnings

Raido Reversed–blockage, problems on trips, resistance to change, reluctance to embrace change, lack of direction or confusion, lack of confidence.

Sowulo (sun)–thunderbolt, power, light, warmth, sense o peace, end of a journey, purpose or triumph.

Sowulo Reversed–No reversal.

Tiwaz (victory)–justice, fairness, honor, sacrifice victory

Tiwaz Reversed–a losing battle, loss of enthusiasm, failure, backstabbing, imbalance, injustice, war

Thurisaz (Thor)–danger, protection, ability to overcome challenges, unwanted circumstances

Thurisaz Reversed–be careful with a decision, betrayal, defenselessness, resistance to change, avoidance

Uruz(power)–strength, power, courage, never-say-die, self-determination, wisdom, growth and change

Uruz Reversed)–loss of strength, determination or health, digging your way out of a hole, in a rut.

Wunjo (joy)–happiness, contentment, joy, positive feelings, sense of contentment

Wunjoy Reversed)–unhappiness, conflict, struggle, Attempt to find happiness.

Pendulums are something attached to a string or chain. When I was pregnant, many women used my wedding ring as a pendulum to see if the baby was a boy or girl. A pendulum can be anything, but many people use crystals. It answers only yes and no, but sometimes other simple answers. You need to be careful. I don't feel these are as accurate as other things, especially if you can do psychokinesis, which means that you can affect and move objects.. You can impose your will on things possibly in that case. The same is downing rods.

Dowsing Rods is a way to get simple yes and no answers. Dowsing rods have always intrigued me. I remember my grandma telling me about people who were dowsers and would find water on people's farms and where to dig. You could count on them to be totally accurate. I sometimes feel that outcomes can be changed, especially if you can do psychokinesis. Pay attention and ask for angel protection first, I always request my guides and angels to surround me first.

One interesting thing about rods is that you can ask a question and get a different answer. Someone else can ask a question, hold them, and get another answer. This is where confidence, and Source come into play. Use rods for a length of time, and they will become imprinted with your energy. You have to trust yourself and have confidence. It's all a part of the process.

Some people believe that since our soul knows everything, that it is actually controlling the answers. Either way can, once the rods are imprinted with your energy, they remain accurate.

Tea Leaves or Coffee Swirls is something I learned from a friend. It's almost like you are using clairvoyance to "see" in the coffee cup. Swirls left mean one thing. Drops, dashes, they all mean different things to different people.

Crystal Balls have been used for thousands of years, and yes, I have one. Be careful if you do buy one to get the real thing, because many are plain glass when they should be real crystal. This is the way you capture energy from the Earth. If I stare at it long enough, I start to see visions in the crystal itself. It acts kind of like a portal.

Dropped eggs in water is a way to read negative energy that has been directed towards you or other people. I've used this in the past to tell if people are trying to do you harm. You wait to see if it separates in water. If it gets stringy, people are trying to do bad to you. If it stays together, then no. At least that is what I was taught. It could be backwards for some people.

Bones are another way that I know how to read. The bones fall into certain patterns that you can read. It's the way they lay that you pay attention to. I usually use animal vertebrae, but there are differing versions.

Iridology is learning to read patterns in the eyes. Some people use this to tell about people's health. I myself have a chart to refer to.

Ouija Boards are something I refuse to mess with. I had some very scary occurrences with boards and refused to play with them. They let in too much energy because the communication can be so extensive. I have many stories about them.

In college, one day my friend pulled out a Ouija board. One of my friends, who was Indian, said he didn't believe it, but my other friend was enamored. We all put our hands on the planchet. When my non-believing friend put his hand on it, it wouldn't move. As soon as he took his hand off, the planchet would move, often faster than we could keep up. We literally watched it move by itself.

It told us that his name was Walter Sjdom. He was murdered on the land we were on. He began to tell us odder things, like he would start speaking German or French, of which both of my friend and I could speak. It started becoming darker every day. He said he had killed people and was giving us names, dates, and then sometimes gibberish. The final straw was when I left the room to take a phone call one evening, and my friend asked the board, "Where is Lana?" The board said, "Let me Check." The planchet flew off the board and hit the door as I opened it. It was one of the few times that I was actually scared.

My husband told me one time his friend was playing with one and burned the tips of his fingers. Neither he nor I will let a Ouija board in the house.

I had another time when a friend of mine threw out her Ouija Board and repeatedly, it kept returning to the house in various ways. It scared the heck outta her. I believe she finally buried it or something.

Be careful of all tools to prohibit negative energy from getting in. They all just need to be respected. Negative energy can come from entities who have not crossed or negative energies who have turned from the light of God. Negative energy can sap your personal energy and wreak all kinds of havoc. To clear energy from the tools after using them, say a prayer something like this;

"Thank you guides, angels and spirits for the information that I have received. Please let me only go good with the messages therein. I now invoke Archangel Michael to remove and protect me from any negative energy and it's effects. Amen."

I personally do not believe in the Devil or demons. I do not believe there are little guys with pitchforks making you do bad stuff. However, I do believe that there are entities who have turned from the light of God for various reasons and drain energy. These people have perhaps not crossed or have made choices that have cut them off from God. You need to be aware and put up your protection. These entities are different from supposed demons; demons were created to do harm on purpose, whereas these entities are just misguided. Entities who are not basking in the light of God are lost and missing out of love. All we can do is keep them from affecting us and pray for them that they come to see the light.

This is Skye and Snickers. My business is named after Skye on the right.

Does Everything Bad HAVE to come in Threes?

You know, I swear it's true. Pay attention and notice if deaths don't come in threes. I swear it does. So not too long after my mother passed, about a year-and-a-half, my grandma died. She was the one a psychic told me I'd be comforting.

My mom's death broke my grandma's heart. She ended up with a rare type of Parkinson's. It broke my heart to see how she went. That night on the day of her funeral, she communicated. As I was falling asleep, I felt a breeze across my face, kinda like someone blew across me. I was becoming more in tune with the energies around me. I wondered if it was my mom, but I'm pretty sure it was her. She was telling me she was OK. I occasionally still communicate with her. She's hanging out with my mom and aunt. When my mom's sister passed recently, I knew she was very excited to be reunited with her. Yes, people wait for our returns. They usually have a big party and celebration on our return.

It was strange to see the order in which these people passed. My grandfather was the oldest and longest lived. At the end, he was miserable. He missed my grandma, had gone pretty much blind, in a home and glad to cross.

He used to ruminate, "I wanna go home!"

Yes, he was right, that is our TRUE home. He passed at 90.

I was never really close with my grandfather, so it was interesting to have so many paranormal occurrences with him. I know I inherited my ability from my mom and wonder often if my ability came from him. He actually popped up more than any other spirit for quite awhile.

The first encounter was at his funeral. I saw him. This was my first actual spirit sighting. I couldn't believe what I was seeing. My grandfather walked into the funeral home, leaned over his body for a moment, and disappeared. He looked young again, like he did in his wedding photo with my grandma. I shook my head. I didn't see that, right? I was the only one?

What I've learned over the years is that we go to our own funerals. I've heard many entities thanking loved ones for flowers or a certain song that was sung during my mediumship sessions. They often thank their loved ones for showing up at the cemeteries. I know that many entities "hang out" with their bodies at the cemetery. This has always intrigued me because it's not the same for cremation. I wanna say that those who have a belief in Christianity do this because they believe in the Second Coming and will reunite with the body. I've seen this sometimes and other times not. I guess it depends on the entity. But entities more often than not show up to see what's going on at their own funeral, offering advice.

We often give those performing the funeral "ideas" of what we'd like done, but we also realize, it doesn't matter, though. Funerals are for the living.

Another thing is that when we cross, we can look anyway we want. Usually we go back to when we looked good, around the age of thirty when we also felt good. As a medium, I've seen both. I've seen some people look young, or some people look about the age when they died when trying to communicate information to a loved on. Most people choose their favorite era, like the '70's feathered hair. I also think some people from the other side are a little vain, showing up when they were at their best. I've also seen spirits come through with the way they wanted to be, like having straight teeth or thick blond hair. It is heaven, I've always guessed, so you get whatever you want. You just wish it.

Another quirky thing that happened after my grandfather passed was that he would appear in pictures. We still have actual photos to this day.

My grandfather was very distinctive. He had alopecia and went totally bald in his thirties. More than once he clearly appeared in a crowd of people who were watching runners competing in the Boston Marathon. At the time, my uncle was running, and we were all so proud he had gotten accepted and finished the Boston marathon. In the crowd of onlookers, we can clearly see him standing among the crowd, cheering everyone. Knowing my grandfather, he would have been proud and happy for my uncle.

I saw the picture, and there was no way it wasn't him. My other uncle said it must've been a coincidence and maybe we had family in the crowd (We live 1,500 miles away).

I always find the skeptics humorous. Everything to them is a coincidence when we all know coincidences don't exist. Everything happens for a reason, and it's in the Book Of Life. Skeptics are always trying to debunk any and all things that are illogical. *Since when is spirit logical?*

You see, as you evolve in your spiritual awakening, you will discover that your reality and perception affect the things you experience. People who don't believe in spirits will never see them. They are closed off to it. I have stood next to nonbelievers and witnessed actual angel, ghosts, and such, even on camera, and they see nothing, even in photos. They have closed off their minds. They have closed their minds to the possibility that maybe, just maybe, there is more out there. Now I am not being judgmental, but I also find most non-believers to think they are also a little smarter than us stupid believers. There's this condescending attitude, not freely expressed, that in some way they are superior, and we are uneducated fools. Well, let them have at it. We have nothing to prove, and if they want to limit their life to the richness of spirituality, let them.

Just like it was a coincidence that my phone rang in the middle of the night, while I was asleep. I picked it up, and it was one of my aunts, whose number I didn't have. She said that I dialed her. I didn't have her number and never picked up the phone. It had been a long time since we talked, and I think my dad may have wanted me to connect again to her.

You see, everything is supposed to work in a certain way. My grandfather knew a picture would be taken. My dad wanted me to reconnect with family. He wanted to relate to everyone he was OK. Maybe it was a message to me. "Yeah, you're not crazy. You saw me."

Something people just really need to wake up! Either way, I truly know that nothing in this life is a coincidence. Nothing.

What The Otherside Is Like

As a medium, I have been blessed to see glimpses of what our home is really like. The spirits on the other side often show me. All I can describe is how it looks to me from an Earthly perspective.

First of all, the colors don't look like the colors here. The colors are more vibrant, to the point of breathtaking. The colors seem to shimmer or vibrate. Green is not green there; it's more than green. The sun seems to be brighter and whiter, but not so much as to blind you. It's like you are a part of the colors, and the colors are a part of you.

Everything on the other side shimmers or vibrates. Every existing thing seems to sing God's praise. Every single thing knows God, and God knows it. . . whether it's people, animals, or even a blade of grass. A tear still comes to my eye as I write this. There just aren't any words for it.

You will meet your friends and family. One of your family or friends has been assigned to help you cross. Many people describe seeing people before they cross: their brother, mother, husband, or wife. This person has been assigned to you to greet you when it is time.

Like I said, there is a big "Welcome Home" party. Now, this may be slightly delayed if you have had a traumatic death. Traumatic death can be described as a lot of pain, or one that has picked up a lot of negative energy. Your soul needs to shed the negativity, so you go to a cocooning chamber to release it. I compare a cocooning chamber to a deprivation chamber here on earth. It's void of everything, so you can just release the negative energy from your soul. I have seen some people be there for a few days, a few weeks, or not at all. It depends. More about that later.

Eventually, we meet everyone we have ever loved here on Earth and in heaven. I find it interesting when people tell me during a reading that they are surprised when their grandmother or great grandmother comes through as a guide for them.

They always say, "I never knew her." Yes, you did. You knew here before you came, and you will know her when you return. Another thing awaiting us are our beloved animals.

Yes, animals go to heaven, just like humans. I find it interesting that there are many biblical verses about animals who have taken human lives and do not enter heaven. Think about it, animals know God. I am an animal communicator. From what I hear from them, it is that they are not afraid to die. They know God. Their body may be afraid physically, but their spirits know where they came from. Animals also understand that they are a part of the circle of life. My chickens know they are food. While I do not eat them, they know why they were created and what their purpose is.

I, at my core, love animals. Maybe that is why I communicate with them. I was taught by my lovely Christian upbringing that animals don't have souls. But they do. As I said before, it's biblical. Animals are pure souls, and I often like them more than I do many humans. I've had many, many animals over the years. I know these animals are waiting for me. I have to chuckle at thinking about all the myriad of animals that will greet me when I pass: every chicken, dog, cat, goat, horse, and parakeet. They wait for us. It's always too bad that we outlive most of our critters. But they understand and wait to be reunited with us.

What I see on the other side when I see animals is that they are all running, flying, and jumping all over the place. They are free to roam and will casually walk by, or a person might pick up and hold their beloved pet. Sometimes they also have their favorite collar on their favorite toy. And just like us, they will be with their best friend, be it a person or other animal.

I've also had a lot of people who have asked about soulmates who are also animals, and yes, it is true, an animal can be a soulmate. I'm not so sure if animals reincarnate, though. I swear sometimes they do. My horse Skye behaves in a quirky manner like my very first horse, Trigger. Trigger had to be put down when he got too old, and I never quite got over it. Skye was born to me a few years later. I know that Skye is a soulmate. I know Trigger is a soulmate, so can they re-incarnate? I think in certain cases, and if not, one horse affects the other. They often become your guides.

I recently had a friend of mine who lost her cat. It was really hard on her, and she felt he was still around her. Yes, they can be guides, and yes, I have actual proof. My friend said she thought she heard her cat in her store one day after he passed. So I turned on my tape on my phone and just let it play. On it very clearly, you can hear a cat meowing! It's on my Social Media. Yes, there is proof animals go to heaven.

How The Other Side Communicates With Me

As of me writing this, I've probably done sixty thousand readings or so. After that, I have learned the symbols, messages, and can translate that for people.

I also read using voice vibration. That's why I use phone readings a lot. It's funny. Sometimes people come in, sit down, and I do what is called a "cold" reading. They give me no information, and I don't need it. Then there are other times people need to talk so I pick up their energy. I've personally noticed that when it rains or snows, I hear a million times better. I figure it's maybe how electricity is conducted through the air. Not completely sure. It's something that I pay attention to.

As for my messages, certain visuals mean certain things. A birthday cake or balloon means a birthday, anniversary, or celebration. I see young children on the other side, holding a grandparent's hand and know they are direct descendants and the person I'm reading for has perhaps miscarried, stillbirth, or terminated. The spirit or energy still says the other side. If the person is holding a baby in their arms, that tells me that there is a baby coming soon. Every medium is different, and there are thousands of examples. Over the years, it's a combination. I've learned my visuals well.

As I said before, I also hear clearly, and sometimes the spirits give me various information. Let me tell you, spirits don't change on the other side. If they were jokesters on Earth, they are still that way on the other side. The only difference that I see in spirits is that there is no stress, depression, or negative emotions. The only sort of negative emotion is regret. Spirits often wish they had done something they haven't or didn't do something they had. They got to see everything they ever did, good or bad. There is a life replay. They got all of eternity to think about it. Most are very regretful, and sometimes will ask for forgiveness from that person on Earth.

One thing that I believe that also happens is that sometimes, people can try to make things right from the other side, kinda like balancing karma in the ethers. I have seen people who were truly nasty and mean to someone try to make things right to that person by guiding or "arranging" good things to happen in a helpful manner to that person on Earth. I believe that not only are these spirits willing to help those they've wronged, I believe it acts as a sort of "brownie point" system of some sort.

Another thing that I find interesting is the earthly people that communicate with me. I am able to communicate with people who are non-verbal and have non-communicative diseases like Dementia and severe Autism. I have also talked to people in comas and related information. Why can I do this? The spirits aren't in their bodies. Some are just walking around, many have already crossed, just waiting for their hearts to stop beating. They always send happiness, contentment and love.

In the Age of Aquarius, Am I Awake or Woke, or Both?

I decided to add this chapter here instead of later in the book because I think what I went through and am still going through is a spiritual awakening. It is a little different than being "woke" but at the same time, alike. I find it interesting that the term "woke" kinda sums up what is going on with someone who has had an awakening. It's a personal and totally spiritual thing—and different for every individual.

Awakenings have been going on forever, but as the planet begins its shift, especially since 2020, there have been more and more "awakenings" as whole soul groups, numbering in the millions, begin to collectively become more spiritual, more connected to who they really are and connected to the collective.

We started the shift into the Age of Aquarius in 2020. Some astrologers say it is not now, but I say it is now. From all the people that I see, it is a massive shift as the planet's vibration and negativity begins to decrease. It's interesting how the COVID pandemic coincided with the beginning of this next twenty-five hundred or so years.

Here are some qualities of the Age of Aquarius. We are leaving the Age of Pisces, or Christianity. I am definitely not leaving Christianity or any other religion totally, but what we are going to be getting away from an organized, controlling religion and realizing that God is within us and that we do not need to be told what to believe or how to believe it.

We are a piece of God; therefore, we are God-like and the purpose of our existence here is how to become God-like as much as possible, so we can return to the Godhead as divine beings.

As Jesus said, in John 8:32, "And you will know the truth and the truth will set you free." This truth is that God is within us, and we need to follow the idea of knowing our own truth. I will write more about this later.

I was raised Christian, but I felt myself more Buddhist in nature. By-the-way, many people don't know that Jesus is mentioned in Buddhism, and it is believed that is where he was during the years 12-31, spending time teaching and learning with Buddha.

Jesus came to me on a Lunar Eclipse in September 2022 and gave me many messages that I will write here later in the book. Jesus has told me that all religions are one, and that there are many ways to God—and at its core is LOVE. Anything in the Age of Aquarius that does not promote love will crumble upon itself. Anything evil will fall apart. That includes the Corporate Systems, the Banking Systems, the governments that want total control and are abusive. I will say it one more time: in the Age of Aquarius, if it doesn't promote love, it will crumble upon itself.

The Age of Aquarius has many components to it. It has Aquarian elements from Astrology. These are some of the things that will be happening and are already happening.

1.   **Increase and Empowerment of Women**–The Age of Aquarius is about women and their divine role in society. It's no longer about the Patriarchy. Now I want to clarify that in no way is this about emasculating men. *Au contraire!* It's about nurturing, caring, and love for others. It's no longer about War. It's about cooperation, caring, and non-violent pursuits. It's no longer about domination, but love. At its core, the Age of Aquarius is about LOVE.

2. **Technology**–The Age of Aquarius is all about the advancement of technology and how to use it effectively to make our lives better. This includes the treatment of disease, mental health, and the security of improving and living with our environment. I am convinced that we are just in our infancy. I think that this technology can be scary for us, but since the Age of Aquarius is about love, we are going to have to trust that things will be the best for the collective.

3. **Cooperation**–Everything in the Age of Aquarius is for the collective and what is the best for everyone. Fair and equal treatment for everyone is part of the Age of Aquarius. I foresee everyone working in small communities to help each other instead of "dog-eat-dog" mentality.

4. **Bartering**–Money will increasingly become less important as we work collectively in communities. I already see this happening. Many people are trading goods with local farmers for food in return for things they may own or services they provide.

   I do see the dollar bill and its components like the Stock Market becoming worthless. I do not know how this will occur. I think it may be gradually as we go more and more to bartering. I think that scares a lot of people, especially Americans who value money so much. Well, I hate to tell you, but money is not that important and that is what is wrong with American Society. Money is way too important. I have things in the Stock Market myself and have not moved it. Again, I think this is all gradual. Could the devalue of money happen suddenly? Perhaps, but I think there is just a realization that what matters is love and people and your planet, those things do not have a price tag.

5. **Environmental awareness**–We will finally begin to realize we are part of the Earth, and respect it and its bounty. I have been predicting for years that here in the United States, the Native American way will gain power as the Native Peoples will gain strength, and we immigrants will finally listen to their ways.

For instance, I truly feel that America's most common protein will once again become the Bison, not the domesticated cow. They are part of the ecosystem and healthier vitamin wise, anyways. Many people don't realize that our lack of Selenium in the United States (which causes thyroid disorders), is directly due to the fact that we are eating domesticated cattle and not buffalo, which has a high amount of Selenium in it.

There will be a drastic increase of Veganism. For me, no matter how much I love animals, I have to eat meat for vitamin reasons. My family genetics have problems with B12 and its absorption. The only way to do this is through animal proteins. My daughter tried to be vegan and ended up nearly in the hospital.

I do see much more local, kinder ways of animals becoming part of the food chain, until we find an answer. That's another thing that will change: the farming of animals. Presently, I go locally for all my food, and as a touch of Native American myself, I ask for the forgiveness of my animal and the thanks that they were willing to give up its life for me. Let's hope in the future with our innovations that maybe technology can find an answer in the next twenty years or so to my body's need for animal proteins. I confidently know that next years will blow our minds, and there will be an answer.

Come on Inner Peace, I don't Have All Day!

You won't believe how many people who call me for a reading are in a spiritual awakening and don't even realize it. They just know something is wrong. One of the most common symptoms is that they feel "stuck."

In the Age of Aquarius, I have seen three distinctive waves of people all collectively awakening. It seems like these people exist as Soul Groups, and they begin their awakening together as we lift the vibration of the planet. It's a collective thing.

There is no way to tell how long it will take for your personal spiritual awakening. Everyone is different. Often, there is more than one. For me, I have had several, but there is usually one big one. Often this is created by an event, often by trauma. For me, I lost my mom. My other ones include hitting my North Node and having a discussion with Jesus. I can guarantee there will be more.

Symptoms of a Spiritual Awakening

After talking to thousands and thousands of people, I can immediately tell when they are having a spiritual awakening. First of all, I can feel it. There is a soul frustration and a "stuck" feeling. These people are carrying it almost as an overlay on their souls.

I always ask them these few questions. By the way, if you can answer yes to half or more of these questions, you are in a spiritual awakening.

1. Do you feel stuck in life?
2. Do the things you used to do seem unsatisfying, or are you bored with your life?
3. Do you need change but don't know how?
4. Is your sleep messed up, needing more or less than before?
5. Have you suddenly become intuitive, having dreams, visions, or premonitions?
6. Have you released relationships with people who do not serve you anymore?
7. Are you having odd physical symptoms like buzzing in the ears, ringing, intense anxiety, or unknown sense of urgency?
8. Are you seeing colors, auras, or lights for no reason?
9. Do you suddenly have tingling or heart palpitations or digestive problems with no known cause?

These are just a few symptoms. Many people may experience one or many of these symptoms. The act of feeling stuck is the most prevalent. Remember, you are becoming a new person through this transition. You will be giving up your old ways and old self.

The best way to start this awakening or even to get the ball rolling is to do something that scares you. This is all about soul growth. You might have to think long and hard about it. I'm not saying to do something like jump out of a plane. There are things that actually can be even scarier.

I had a client that I told this to. She was being tortured by a narcissistic ex-husband. He was stalking her and sending threats on her Social Media, even though she blocked him. He was showing up at her work. I asked her what really scared her. She thought for a moment, and thoughtful replied,

"Standing up to my ex, looking him in the eye, and telling him that he can do nothing to hurt me anymore."

Wow, how powerful is that? Even in her trauma and PTSD, she was able to think of it. She has not finished it yet. She is working on it. I know she had actually told him no and put a restraining order on him. Talk about leveling up!

My suggestion is to start small if you are not able to make big moves. Make small changes at first. We know change is hard, especially for some people. Eat a new food, drive a different way home or take up a new hobby. Every small change you do makes it easier to make the bigger changes, until you are ready for the bigger transitions. Making small changes leading to bigger ones and also gives people confidence that "yes" I can do it. It depends on the person.

There are seven stages of your spiritual awakening. I will be writing more about this later because it is a book all by itself! No one goes through the stages cleanly.

You will go through the stages Level 1 or 2, go back to 1, go through 3 or 4, go back to 2, and so forth. Notice how close these are to the stages of grief. You are grieving the old you. You are grieving time lost not being the real you. You may have several smaller versions or one big awakening. Everyone is different.

Level 1: The "stuck" Phase. Often being in a "rut" or feeling general malaise. These are the feelings that you may be experiencing.
- Unhappiness with your life
- No direction
- Needing change and not knowing how
- Feeling empty
- Feeling feeling lost
- Having a feeling, "This is all there is?'

You have to do something. If you don't it will be done for you. Here it comes.

Level 2: The Tower Card. Unless you make some type of change and quit resisting change, the change will be made for you by the Universe. The Tower Card in the Tarot deck is the card of dramatic, sudden change. It can be catastrophic at times.
- Usually happens quickly
- May be Shocking
- Usually traumatic
- Life-changing

This leads us to the next level, ouch.

Level3: Shock and Disbelief. This phase is going to leave you reeling, feeling completely drained. Some feelings you may feel:
- Disbelief
- My life is no longer real
- WHY ME?
- Is this really happening?

You have to be very careful not to feel sorry for yourself at this level.

Level 4: Anger. You are just plain angry. There may even be no apparent reason. You may take things out on other people—or even blame them for your problems. Here are some thoughts and emotions:
- Anger at yourself for putting up with everything and allowing yourself to get into the situation.
- Anger at yourself for wasting all this time and precious energy.
- Anger at those who have wronged you.
- Anger at being pushed forward.

The next level is the toughest to get through, trust me.

LEVEL 5: The Dark Night of the Soul. This is where you soul grows the most, often by leaps and bounds. These symptoms are the part of the journey that I was talking about before. These symptoms include:
- Anxiety
- Depression
- Buzzing sensation
- Need to get rid of people who no longer serve you
- Unwillingness to be around "phony" people. These people may be friends of family that you have known for years.
- Heart palpitations
- Sudden awareness of gifts you knew you never had, like clairvoyance.
- Intense dreaming.
- Crying.
- Sudden altruistic attitude
- Rage
- Euphoria
- Tingling somewhere on the body, usually hands or feet
- Visions of Angels or family member
- Insomnia or extreme tiredness
- Stomach Ache
- Ability to assess a person or situation immediately
- Deep need to understand and grasp the concepts of spirituality
- Gain or lose weight

The next one I call a form of Processing.

Level 6: Processing/Accepting Ownership. These symptoms might include:
- Searching, finding and understanding your purpose
- Understanding and knowing that there is something much greater than you, and appreciating it.
- Let Go and Let God
- Definite increase in Faith
- Calmness in your soul begins to occur
- Gratefulness
- Appreciation
- Develop the ability to meditate and communicate with your higher self
- Appreciation and even greater level for alone time and nature
- Learning to trust your gut feelings and decisions

Level 7: Alignment and Acceptance. You are literally pulling out of the awakening and realigning with the real you.
- A good flow of energy, things feel right
- Things seem to manifest
- Decisions become easier
- Magical things seem to happen
- A contentment seems to settle within your soul.
- The vibration of your soul seem to raise.
- Petty things that seemed to bother no long are a problem.

Remember, you can go back and forth between these phases several times. There is no time limit. But when you are done, you will know. You can never see the forest through the trees when you are standing in the forest!

Living In 5D: SO the Resonance Hertz?

So, let me explain this. We start our current lives in 3D. That is currently our reality: length, width, depth. We are selfish, have egos, are competitive, and experience negative emotions such as jealousy, envy, hate, fear, and worry. We know that through intentions and hard work, we manifest and manipulate our surroundings. This is our reality of Earth in its present tense.

As we have our spiritual awakenings, we are going into 4D, and together, also lifting up the resonance of the planet. Many theologians think that the afterlife is actually 4D. That's why so many people are starting to communicate with their ancestors There is no need for greed, selfishness, hate, jealousy, or disdain. Everything you could want is there, but there is much, much more to it. Even our ability to manifest grows exponentially.

People coming into 4D are beginning to realize that there is more to life than materialism, competition, and these beings begin to understand oneness with everything in the Universe. Since people who are heading into 4D are also self actualizing (being all that they can be), they are realizing that they have the ability to access and use manifestation to let our needs be met also. Everything that they need or desire is at their fingertips. They are learning to obtain anything and everything.

Empathy, love, and oneness are those experiences and become what our soul craves. The Earth becomes more important, and it's care is imperative. Kindness and altruism become our desires to get to that special place, 5D or the 5th dimension.

This is where true love and happiness comes from. This is where loving the collective, kindness, and true selflessness come from. It's no longer caring about society and its restraints. No one is saddled with guilt or peer pressure. No one cares what others think. It is light and carefree. It's actually how spirituality truly operates. It's oneness with God. Some people call it True Freedom, some people call it Nirvana, or Kundalini. There are many names for it.

I compare it to a perpetual state of meditation. For me, when I meditate, the feeling of the 5th Dimension occurs when I am using my Theta waves.

Our brain waves are usually functioning in alpha or beta waves. This is our conscious thoughts here on the planet. Theta waves are a higher level, Christ Consciousness wave that kinda feels like when you meditate and just for a little bit, if even a few seconds, like you are off the planet. No one can get to you. No worries, no anxiety, no pressure. This is the state your soul wishes to be perpetually. It's what we strive for. Getting there and staying there are two different things.

As human beings, even as we evolve, people cannot stay in 5D. It is virtually impossible. We get worried, lose our tempers, and let our egos get the better of us. The thing is: that's what we should be trying to do. No ego, no anger, no negativity of any kind. That sounds nearly impossible, right? Well, that's what we all should be striving for. I'm writing another book about how to keep yourself in Christ Consciousness. I know, it's hard. It's something to ascertain.

Don't Come a Knockin' when the Beings Come a Rockin'

This was about the time that I really started seeing things. Angels, orbs, etc. I began attracting them and still do. Being a Sagittarius, we are not only lucky, but extremely spiritual. I have this habit of rubbing off on people. Literally my luck becomes their luck. But also in the paranormal realm. People have weird experiences when they are around me. This can even be verified by viewers who have watched me live when they see orbs, or whatever else shows up on a camera.

Well, my husband started to have odd occurrences. He often doubted my encounters. When I met him, he was an atheist. Well, not anymore. You see, he was always turned off to things as being impossible, I just showed him differently.

A lot started after my mom's death. I will never forget him waking me up one night in a dead panic.

He sat straight up in bed, screaming, "What WAS that?"

I sat up also.

"What?" I responded sleepily.

"I saw this light, this round light. It hovered over you, then bounced down the hall, and disappeared. I saw it." He still couldn't believe it.

"I don't know, maybe my mom, a guide, or Something."

I was used to this all by now, so I rolled over and went back to sleep. He, however, did not go back to sleep. It unnerved him. After a few days, he finally accepted the possibility that maybe, just maybe, this stuff Is real. Simply, his eyes were opened. And that orb was just the beginning.

Throughout the rest of the years in our house, it seemed to become like a train station of the paranormal: we saw spirits, heard noises, and saw seven-foot-tall angels walk through walls. I believe to this day that I unknowingly opened a portal somehow. I was bombarded often, but I also now realize that my spiritual awakening had opened a floodgate—and this is normal. Remember that nothing about this is truly abnormal, especially during a time of rapid spiritual development. This was about the time that I started having very vivid dreams of me being on the otherside. One dream was similar to one of my followers, but with a small twist.

So my dream was from the other side. There was a man there, who I think I know, but yet, I didn't. I felt like I knew him though. I kneeled in front of him, and he knighted me with a sword, and said, "You've been chosen." It feels like I understood at the time but woke up confused.

A few months later, in another dream, I was on a hill. I was next to a man. I feel like he was wise, like he was God or Jesus. I looked out, and all I could see were thousands of people. Rows and rows of people.

Once again, I heard, "You have been chosen." I felt responsible for these people. I was responsible to get God's message to them. You are loved. You are infinite. You are a piece of God. These many faces would become the people on my Social Media.

I would also like to say, all of this is nothing to be scared of. I know it can be quite overwhelming but trust me, after a while it becomes old hat.

If you are still afraid, remember you can control it. Like I said to many, many of my mentors and followers. You can control all of this. Remember, you have more energy. You are alive, they are dead. Say a prayer of protection to your guides and angels, or even ask God to remove them until you are ready. Maybe say something like this:

"Thank you God for blessing me with the presence of all of these beings of the heavenly realm. Please keep me calm and do not let me experience anything that I cannot handle."

Beings are there for a reason. Then again, you may not even have this "problem." It's not actually all it's cracked up to be. Everyone is different and on their own course.

I also often get questions from parents who want to help their children who are afraid of what their children are seeing. Most of these kids are scared of beings, spirits, etc. Remember little ones are still acclimating into this life and remember the otherside clearly. Go ahead and ask a child under four, and they will tell you who they are and what they did before they were who they are now.

It was about this time that I decided to get Past-Life Regression. After talking to my daughter, I was sure this was real. So I made an appointment with a local hypnotist (This person was associated with the person that I eventually got trained through).

If you have never had a Past-Life Regression, I will once again say that I highly recommend it. It is truly life changing. Not only do you realize you are eternal, but you start to recognize people in this lifetime who you knew before and how they interact in this lifetime.

You see, we have a soul family of about 2,500 people. These are all soulmates. We can interact with people outside of our circle, but these people are those we have interacted with the most. And of the 2,500, there are about 100 that have a very similar imprint and very closely match our vibration. We have spent so much time with them that we are very similar. This is created by karma, both good and bad.

Past-Life Regression changed my life. The therapist began by addressing, like I said before, any lingering past-life issues affecting my current life. For me, I had a deep fear of tornadoes. As a three-four year old, if my mother even mentioned a tornado watch, I was in the bathroom throwing up. It was beyond terrifying for me.

In regression, I must've been a man. I could see my hands were large and rough. I wore a red flannel shirt and could see my cuffs. I was in Nebraska, finishing a house. I was going to send for my family soon. A tornado came and destroyed everything I had worked so hard for. I died, clinging to a tree on my knees. I remember being not so mad at dying, but mad that I had worked so hard and had it ripped from me (another ongoing theme in my life).

Some other things I saw: Years ago, maybe the Stone Age, my current husband was my brother. Our parents died and I had to take care of him. I remember ducking behind rocks to hide from another competing tribe. My brother (husband) wouldn't shut up, and I was scared we'd be found. I do not know what happened after that, but I'll never forget the vividness of the colors of the rocks. They shimmered, much like the colors from the otherside. I am told that when the colors are that vivid, you learned what you needed from that lifetime, and the lifetime lesson is complete.

I saw myself as a female Native shaman who raised horses. I was giving this beautiful chestnut paint a bath in the creek. On the other side of this creek was a steep embankment. I was washing and rinsing this horse. I never knew this until a few years later, many Native American women were not only shamans, but raised horses as well. I knew I raised a type of horse that doesn't exist anymore. It was a mix of Paint horse and Appaloosa. I had to look this all up, but yes, it's true. And I was born with a love for horses that has never left, especially American breeds. And as a Shaman, I think this is why I know herbs so well to this day. Maybe that's why I am studying herbalism.

One of the last lifetimes that I found the most disturbing was the wagon going West. I was only around two and in a Reed basket where I starved to death. My parents had gotten smallpox and died, but I did not catch it. I starved.

One of my saddest memories was when I was an alcoholic Madam at a brothel during the Gold Rush. I remember seeing myself in the mirror with bright red hair. I died of liver failure. I was only forty-seven. It was a bleak, depressing existence. I did what I had to do. I was hoping for riches and ended up miserable. To this day, I have never been to California and always refused to go for some reason. Now I know why. Maybe one of these days I will force myself to go.

We can break out of some of these negative patterns if we are aware and make the effort. I swore to myself to not be afraid of tornadoes. Simple say to yourself: "That was then, this is now. I'm not dying in this way."

Seldom do we repeat a past pattern in that way. I took the bull by the horns and now am a weather spotter.

Is it Soulmate or Soulfate?

After my Past-Life Regression, I began recognizing people. I could place them in other lifetimes. One of them is a major player who is one of my guides yet today. Jack (name changed) was a holistic practitioner who I needed to see for my cross-bite. My jaw shifted my neck vertebrae and caused me headaches. He was just down the street, so I began visiting him often for adjustments. I never realized this, but most of the time, soulmates recognize you, too.

Thinking back, Jack knew who I was to him. I remembering him saying to me: "Yeah, my last name is _____. It's Greek."

He was subtly telling me his name was different in this life and that he had chosen it. Thinking back, that was exactly what he was saying. "Hey look, this is who I am THIS time!"

I really liked him. Didn't know why. He was married and had some kids, so did I (It was always platonic). It all was good until the visions came. And came outta the blue.

I became friends with his secretary first. This was when I was first starting to read for people. She had me read for her, and she was surprised at the accuracy. Then she had Jack sit down for a reading. His secretary made him.

Let's just say, I've never seen such a shocked expression on someone's face. And let's just say I kept him from making some very bad decisions. He thanked me for the rest of his life, and gave me lots of business references.

This is where I started to see the connection. Yes, I knew him. And I got verification that I wasn't making it up. It came to me one day while I was meditating.

Years ago, there were women called courtesans. They are basically play-toys for wealthy men. That's what I was, but I'd call it a "kept" woman. In this other life, I was Jack's side piece. I was short, petite, and had dark hair. I wore green crushed velvet and owned a small black pony that matched his horse. Jack was the lord of the manor. He was very wealthy and had tall boots and rode a Friesian black horse. He owned a large brick manor.

In one instance in that life, I remember never fitting in and trying to go to the kitchen with the other servants. They were sitting at a round table, talking. I saw Jack's now present secretary as a housekeeper sitting there and a friend named Jan in this life who was a cook. It seemed strange that she would be there. I found out later that my friend Jan, even though she lived far away, actually went to Jack as a client. I was floored and that told me that I wasn't making things up.

I mentioned it one time to Jack and how we knew each other. He mentioned tall boots, too. Yeah, he remembered. He had a lot of intuition and used it but didn't realize it.

We held a platonic client/homeopathic clinician relationship for years until his passing. I haven't been able to find anyone like him and miss him even today.

Of all people, I was the one he called when he was dying. He called me several times, much to the chagrin of his wife. He was scared, but he knew. Yes, he knew. After his death, within a few days, he appeared to me. He sat on a chair, casually drinking a martini.

He said to me, "I can still practice my craft through you."

He has become a guide and gives people herbal remedies when I channel. He has appeared several times in my lives behind me as a shadow and has actually taken over a Reiki session, picked up crystals and caused them to float in midair. Yeah, he just wants me to realize he's there. Even through all of this, I still miss him.

One thing people need to understand that even though we can see or feel our loved ones after their passing, it's still not the same as when they were alive. It's just not the same. I was depressed and anxious after his death. I needed more spiritually to help make sense of it all. My talent and purpose was to bring comfort through my mediumship, and I couldn't bring it to myself.

Is Destiny a Playboy?

Around this time, I found out my dad had cancer. He had gotten a lung transplant, and the transplant had cancer in it. He told me in August, and he only lived until Mother's day of the next year. I tried to be there when we put him in hospice. It was hard. I still had kids at home and drove over thirty-five minutes nearly daily to see him and bring him things he needed.

We decided to put him in hospice instead of leaving him at home. He wanted to be at home. We knew it, but he needed too much care. It's always a hard decision. I don't judge anyone having to make that decision. It's a tough one. We do the best we can.

I was there when he died. I had never actually been in a room when someone died. He was desperately trying to stay alive until my brother got there, but I let him talk to my brother on the phone, then I told dad it was OK to go. He smiled and left.

I believe he saw my mom. He said he had seen her. That's how to tell when people get ready to pass. They start seeing dead loved ones. I had a dream also where my grandfather and great grandfather were in a photo frame, smiling at me. I understood this as that they were going to greet him when he crossed. I think my mom was in that room. I also felt a presence, and it seemed like angels.

I believe my mom was there. I'd like to explain that. Just because they were married, they don't necessarily spend eternity together. My parents never are seen together on the other side. I've also never seen my grandparents together. The karma and agreement was met. They have other things to work on. They may meet each other, but most entities have more spiritual endeavors like studying or planning their next lifetimes. I've seen many couples together at times, but what I've seen most often is a mother and son together or daughter-mom or daughter-father. It's who you have the strongest link to. I see my mother and grandmother together often.

After my dad's death, I waited to hear from him. You see, sometimes you hear from them immediately, sometimes you don't. It depends on how much trauma was involved in the crossing and inviting was easy. My dad was sick, so it was awhile before I heard.

When people have a rough crossing, they are put in a "cocoon" to release the negative energy. I liken it to a deprivation chamber. They are there until they feel better. Kind of like a nice long sleep.

It was about six weeks before he came to me in a dream. He was fly-fishing (he loved to fish). He turned to look at me, and he was young. As he made a silly face at me, I then woke up.

The next morning, my eldest daughter called. She had the exact same dream. That's how I knew he had made it and was doing well.

After that, we moved to our farm. It was not uncommon to smell cigarettes (he smoked) everywhere, including in the car and sometimes one of my daughters could smell it at the same time and be an hour away. I'm still not sure how entities do it, but they can indeed be in more than one place.

Matter-of-fact, my dad used to think he was funny by "doing things." One night, it was about 2:00 a.m. and I couldn't sleep. I was watching TV and could smell cigarettes.

"Whoever is here, let your presence be known," I said aloud.

To this day, it freaks me out. My TV came on, turned off, turned on again, then flipped off. Yeah, it was my dad. I know I deal with this everyday, but I still find things that surprise me.

Old McLana Had a Farm

I always wanted a farm as far back as I could remember. I wanted my horses with me. I had two horses and had boarded them for several years (What a pain but that's a whole other story). It was odd how it all happened, but I just went with it and trusted my gut and Higher power—and it all worked out.

It all started with my husband's horse, Misty. We bought her from someone. She got a tendon injury before we even bought her. My husband thought he could help her. I tried to tell him that she wouldn't get better. When horses get injuries like hers, they just don't get better. But he loved that horse. We spent a lot of money trying to treat her, from chiropractors to shoes. She was special and well loved. Her injury got to the point of manageability.

Horses are kinda like cars. You can't drive a car with a flat tire, and you can't ride a horse with a hurt leg. Her leg never got better. But we did get the most important thing from her. We decided to breed her. Everyone told us she couldn't get pregnant, but she did.

I think I inherited my talent for breeding horses from my dad's father. He raced horses. He also had a knack for fixing horses with injuries. He had an uncanny sense for what was wrong with a horse (sound familiar?). He was often able to get the horse running again and then would turn around and sell them.

I knew what I wanted. I bred Misty to a black and white Paint. I needed a good minded, a little stocky, gentle but smart horse.

The problem with Misty was that in her breeding, because she was a halter horse used for shows. She had very neat lines and small feet, which caused her injuries. In people it's kinda like fasciitis; your feet aren't big enough for your body. So when I bred her, I made sure of sound feet, a decent body, and nice coloring. I got everything I wanted, and then some.

When we bought Misty, we were told that she couldn't get pregnant. A vet owned her and tried to breed her repeatedly, but nothing took. We bred her one time, and it took. I'll never forget when my Twin Soul palpated her which was to check for pregnancy. We already knew. She was acting differently. She was quieter and gentler.

My husband and daughter had such a special bond with her. The vet said Misty hated men. That was far from the truth. She loved my husband to death. They lived for each other until the end.

Skye was born within a month of us buying our hobby farm. We waited and waited. Ever hear of the expression, "A watched pot never boils?" Well, a watched horse often does not like to give birth in front of people. I swear a mare will hold that foal in until a person isn't watching. I didn't have a camera at the time, so we waited. Finally, one morning, Misty came to get hay and running behind her was a gangly looking foal.

Within a few days, I knew something was wrong. Skye appeared sick. He ended up having an infection. He wasn't getting enough antibodies in her milk. He nearly died. I remember carrying him to the barn and nursing him to health. Yeah, he's now 1,200 pounds. He still thinks in his mind that he's one hundred and twenty-five pounds.

The bond we have with horses is different than with dogs and cats. The understanding is that horses are big enough to kill you if they wanted. And yet, they let you ride them, train them, and listen to you also. As an animal communicator, horses understand that humans are smarter than they are. They understand that they should be guided by us, and that we are the leaders. Skye understood that from birth. He still thinks that he is a young foal. Even to this day, all I have to do is raise my voice, and he puts his head down. It took him four years of bonding with him until I was able to ride him. I love him to death. His mother never saw him to maturity.

When Skye was about eighteen months, Misty tore a tendon so badly we knew what we had to do. My twin soul came out to put her down. We euthanized her right there in the field. Skye watched her mother die. Animals know. If you think for one moment that animals don't grieve, guess again.

I've never seen a grown man cry like my husband did when that horse died. He was lucky enough to find another horse that he had for many years, but it wasn't the same.

Skye grew into a great horse for me. He reminded me of my last horse, Trigger. I am convinced Trigger came back to me through Skye. He has a lot of the quirks that Trigger used to do, that most horses don't do.

I think God sends us our animals. I truly also believe that animals return because of their love for us. Animals are a blessing from God.

Yes, farms are a lot of work, but I feel that I was blessed by it. The way it came into our lives was uncanny. Land has a soul to it. My land had deep Native American connections to it, and I have been entrusted with it. I think the former owner selected me, in a way.

A Farm Haunting

The former owner haunts my property but not in a bad way. She lived there for many years. She appears a lot, not so much in recent years, though. More than once, a friend or client said there is a lady looking out through the window at her. She appeared so often that she scared my kids to death.

When we first moved in, she would call their names from downstairs, but no one was there. One day my middle daughter came running upstairs, shaking. She went up to the mirror, and looking back at her was an old lady.

Well, that was enough of that. I decided to clear the house. This is the way to do it.

I didn't even sage the house. I simply walked into every room, stating loudly that she is to stop scaring my children. She is welcome to stay if she follows the rules. If not, I will make her leave. She has been very respectful to my kids since, acting almost as a protector.

Remember, as I have stated before, I am alive, she is dead. You have more energy and can control the situation. We have this house now and promise to take care of the land.

Ghosts aren't what you think. They are not like in the movies. I have yet to be scratched, hit, or anything else done to me. I've cleaned hundreds of houses, with no problem. I just ask for my angel protection and proceed on my way.

I personally have had no problems with my house since. I truly believe that the owner has become a protector. To this day, she has never bothered my kids again. However, unsavory friends of my children are another story. Remember, I told my ghost to stop bothering my children, and she did. Other people staying at my house is quite another story.

My middle daughter used to have a bad habit of hanging out with questionable people at times. The only time any sightings of "things" around my house have appeared was when people, who shouldn't have been around, were hanging out. I have numerous stories, one of them about a famous entity.

The Beast of Bray Road is a werewolf-like beast of international fame. There are movies made about it. It is a creature that is about seven feet tall, dark, wolf-like with red glowing eyes. It is found usually at night, sometimes eating or scaring motorists. There have been many, many sightings throughout the years. Not so much near where I live, but there have been some strange sightings that I have heard about in recent years that were suspect.

The main place of sightings is in Elkhorn, Wisconsin, which is about thirty miles from me. That is close, so I believe what these people have told me. Like I said, I have never seen it but heard it. This is story one.

So, a good friend of my daughter used to stay overnight. At that time, the only way to get to my apartment in the basement was to go completely through the house. So, to keep things quiet, my daughter and her friends would go through an escape recessed window. This friend also smoked, and she knew that I didn't like smoking in my house.

She told me she saw this wolf-thing right by the window when she came outside. It was really tall, about seven feet, was on all fours, and had a real tall back hump with black spiky hair. Its eyes glowed red. She was so scared that she jumped back through the window and refused to go that way again. When she told me, she hesitated because she didn't think I'd believe her.

I'm not sure if she saw The Beast of Bray Road, or what some people call a Hellhound. I often think they are protectors in some way, though.

The second sighting came about two years later. I would like to say, that neither of these two people knew each other.

My daughter was dating a guy that my ghost seemed not to like also. He had a lot of activity around him. I know my former owner especially took a disliking to this guy. She knew he was no good. She used to torment him; scratching at walls from the outside on a basement wall (think about how that's not possible; dirt on the other side of the wall). It had him so unnerved that he decided to drive home one night early.

It was about 1:30 a.m. As he was driving, he saw what he described as a "demon" of about seven feet tall, standing on two legs, spiky black hair, and red glowing eyes.

He freaked out and drove ninety miles an hour to the end of the road. Here's where it gets even weirder. He saw the "beast" again. This brings up a question as to whether there is more than one or can the beast dissipate and reappear.

He drove home, he told his mom, and they recorded his testimony on tape. He was so scared he refused to come back ever.

What I believe: the beast as well as the former owners are some kind of protector. I have slept many times in a tent in my own backyard. No problems. It does seem like when "they" don't like someone, they will do "things."

One morning, while I had never seen it, I definitely heard something. I almost wanna say it let me hear it on purpose.

It was at daybreak several months later, and I was near my barn and heard something that sounded like a cross between a roar and an animal eating something. It was definitely no coyote. Coyotes were so bad by the house. It would surprise many of you, but it was NOT a coyote.

I have to admit the sound was bone chilling. But oddly enough, I was not and am not afraid. They are there to protect me and understand that I am there to take care of my land . . . my native American land that I have been entrusted to.

Not only that, but like I said before, I have been Native American before and am really drawn to the culture. Many of my psychic friends have also told me that they feel a calming, but heavy Native American influence on my property. Just down the road within walking distance are nine burial mounds. I believe my land may have been a meeting place

I try hard to use no pesticides and do everything as organic as possible. I hope my ancestors are pleased.

When The Most Haunted Location Is in Your Own Backyard

E ver notice every single haunted place in the world is always deemed the "most haunted place in the world" or the most "haunted place in America?"

Wisconsin has been many notorious places for hauntings, including the place of Native Mounds (I found most Native Mounds to be calm and peaceful). But never, ever have I been to a place as haunted (active) as a place called Weary Road near Evansville, Wisconsin. This place even has its own website. I also gave this place its own chapter.

My run-in with Weary Road started around 2008 or 2009. Cameras on phones were just becoming a thing, so I still had a small digital camera that seemed to catch orbs, lights, and such.

No one knows quite how Weary Road got its reputation, or even how it got its haunting, but here are some of the stories.

Many years ago, there was a house on a curve on Weary Road. The old man who lived there was a pedophile and used to lure kids to the house. Supposedly the town found out and were going to lynch him. He killed himself, six kids, and burned down the house. There were a couple of other stories, but that was one I got.

All I know is that I've never seen a more haunted location, I have interacted with ghosts and spirits more than ten times there. So often have I caught things on camera, but I've lost photos.

The first time I went there was with my middle daughter and some of her friends. I caught tons of orbs, and a photo of "little people" inside my car.

There is a story out there that when you stop your car on this little bridge, the car won't start. There is this photo, and there are these little beings that look like the guy from the AOL logo (remember?). They are all over my dashboard.

You can see their reflections in the dashboard

It took me awhile to figure out what they were. I finally asked one of my Native American friends who nonchalantly told me they were wood nymphs, that live in the trees and often wreak havoc on humans.

At that time, I also caught tons of green streaks in the total darkness, and thousands of moving orbs. I found out that bright green streaks are ribbon energy, and all of the orbs are coming and going. This place is known as a portal.

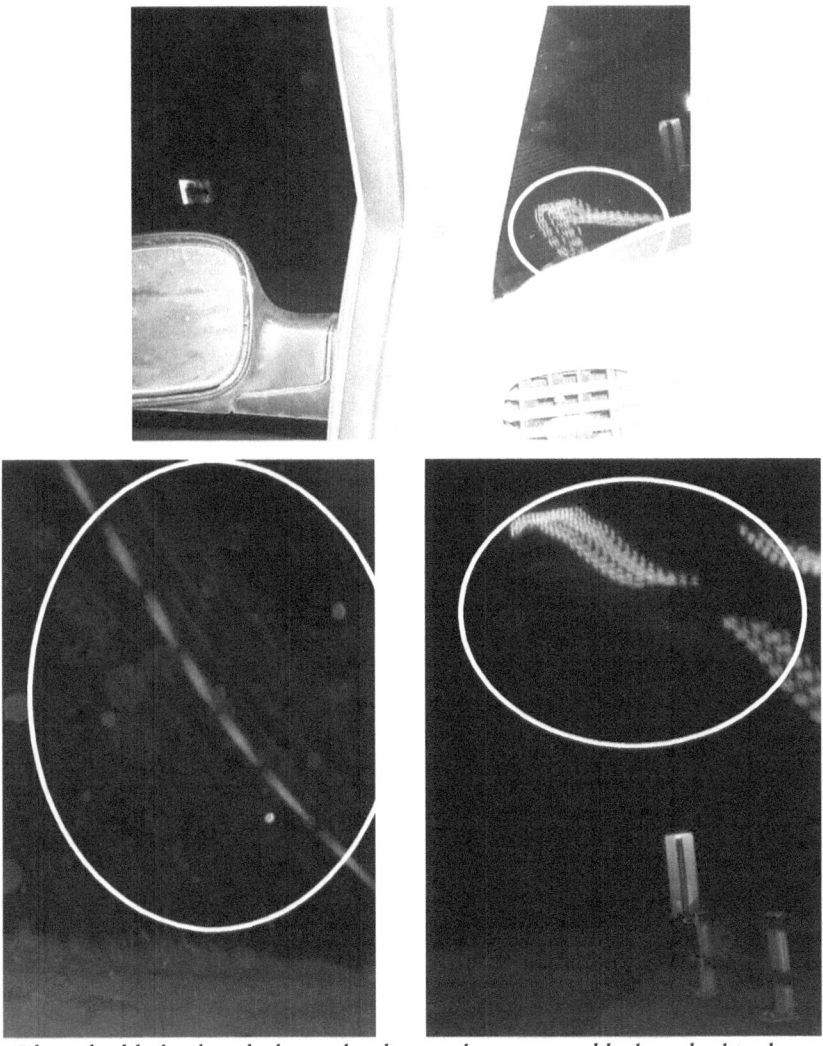

I have highlighted with the circles the streaks since it is black and white here.

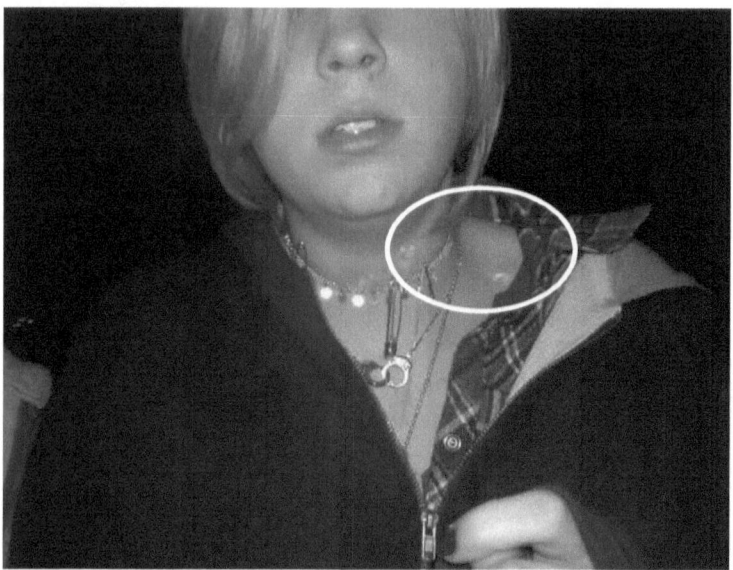

Five small lights are on her neck

This was also the time, when my daughter said she felt like something was choking her. I took a photo, and on top of her head, a small yellow light sits on her head, and on her neck, five small lights are on her neck. Wood nymphs, fairies? It really freaked her out. She won't go back.

But unlike her, my curiosity got the best of me. I took several friends. This is where I picked up another of my guides. I have eight to ten guides.

I had told my friend about how haunted this place was, and she wanted to go. You can't see anything during the day, so we waited until night for things to show up. Um, yeah . . .

We parked our car, and I just sat. Now at this time, I was still developing my mediumship abilities. I didn't see entities yet, but I could hear and feel them.

As we sat, my friend's eyes got really big.

"Look, there's a guy standing next to our car. He wants to know why we are here. He looks like he's on fire."

I could feel something, so I started snapping pictures. Yes, there is a floating head and a picture of a man with a hat on. He looked like he was on fire.

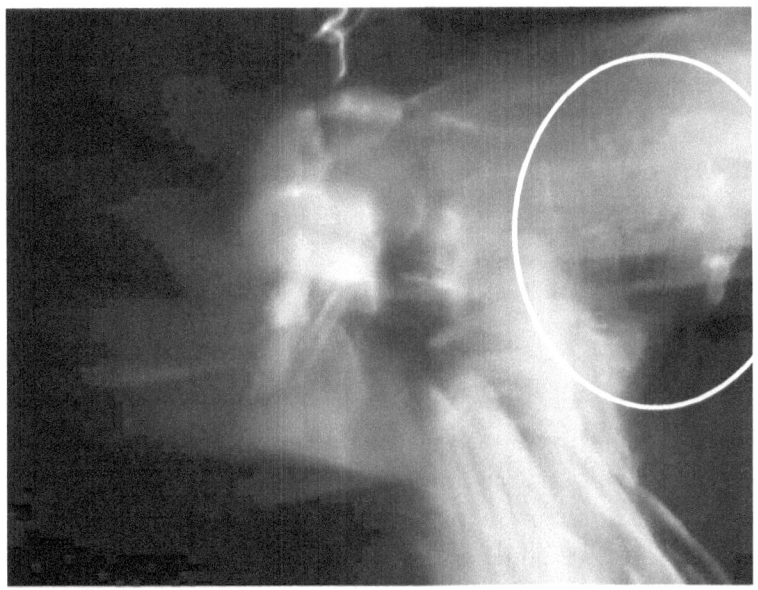

My photo of Jim. Notice his face, beard and hat?

All I could say was, "His name is Jim. He's stuck here."

I said a prayer to Michael the Archangel to come and get him and bring him to the otherside.

We actually were too scared to get out of the car this time to walk, especially my friend, who wanted to leave. I thought nothing of this so we left.

I had a dream that night that I will never forget. I am on a marble staircase. It had big columns. Staring and smiling at me was a man. I smiled back.

He mentally said to me, "Thanks for helping me cross. I'm Jim. I'm going to help you all I can from this side."

I realized that I was in heaven, and I was at the Hall of Records. The Hall of Records is a record of everything we've ever said, did or even thought. We can learn there, too. It's one of the first place we return to on the other side. Then I realized I had to go back to Earth. Jim could stay, and I couldn't. I was angry and saddened. I didn't want to go back.

My husband woke me from my dream and said I was sobbing. Yeah, Earth sucks. But I know I have things to do here yet.

I also love when I get confirmation about all this stuff. Even as a psychic, you can doubt things. Confirmation of all that happened came about nine months later, via one of my followers.

She called me outta the blue.

"I remember the story you told me about the guy on Weary Road. I want to share this article with you that I found in the newspaper."

She proceeded to read to me about a man who was burning leaves in the 1980s and died when he caught his shirt on fire. He lived on Weary Road. His first name was Jim.

Definite confirmation.

I had another episode out there, where our camera lights would answer questions by blinking yes or no questions, and another where one of my followers got scratched on his neck. It took months to heal.

Like I said before, that's one thing that I have to say, I have never been touched by an entity. I truly believe that they are not allowed. I have been told by another medium that I am pretty spiritually strong, and they are not either allowed to—or are afraid to. I do always say a prayer before entering this situation, so my guides are with me also. Ask and you shall receive.

Here's a prayer you can use that might help:

Heavenly Source,

I call on you for protection as I go into this situation with love and life. Protect me with my guides and angels.

Amen.

I think the strangest episode on Weary Road was when I brought seven people with me one night to the bridge. It was near Halloween. Everyone got out of the car.

I heard my good friend at the time say, "Did you see that?'"

I turned around and at my feet was a tabby cat. In the middle of nowhere at 11:00 p.m. (I might like to add that people used to do cat sacrifices on the bridge near there.)

"I saw it. I saw it. It came from under the bridge. It was big like the size of a tiger, but now it's normal sized."

One of the women bent down and petted it. I say it because it was definitely no cat. It was a spirit and pure energy. Within ten minutes, the woman was throwing up. She had to get into her car and leave. Everyone was freaked out.

I didn't pet the cat, but I did say, "Oh, kitty, I'd take you with me if I could. It actually tried to climb into my car. I got out and turned around. The cat was gone.

Since I was the only one left, I drove home. My husband was asleep, and I went to bed. I thought nothing of it.

In the morning, my husband made a comment that I will never forget.

"I don't know why, but I swear there was a cat in bed with me all night, rubbing up against me."

Oops. I accidentally brought it home. I had invited it. That's something that I have learned quickly. You can get attachments. You can invite them, or they can just follow you. My middle daughter brought home an entity who had committed suicide. He had a blue jean jacket on and dressed like the '80s.

I am better aware of attachments now and usually cleanse myself after clearing any areas.

If you do ever end up with something following you around, just say a prayer of protection to Michael the Archangel. Then demand them to leave.

How do you know if you might have something following you around? Here's a short list. There might be more, but these a few the most important.

1. You feel "off" but can't quite put your finger on it.
2. You feel drained, exhausted or have lost ambition.
3. Weird things keep happening. Things suddenly disappear and reappear, like cellphones, money, etc.
4. You keep waking up at night for no reason.
5. You have bad dreams or night terrors.
6. It seems like one bad thing after another happens.
7. You "see" someone out of the corner of your eye.
8. Animals seem to stare at something that isn't there when around you.

Do not forget that you can have good people hanging out with you like your ancestors also. These people are there to help. Their energy is loving and kind. We don't want them gone. We want to recognize the straggler, the lost, the negative entities, the ones that seem to suck your energy gone.

This is a time to mention too, not to think that your streak of what you would call "bad luck" is a negative entity. Sometimes, bad things happen to good people (remember, you planned it!). The negative energy seems to kinda linger. Just pay attention, and if in doubt, just clear your energy with prayer and some sage.

Remember, you are alive, they are dead. You have more energy and are more powerful. Take control.

Why was 6 Scared of 7? Because 7 Ate 9

After the death of a lot of my family, I went through a period of deep longing and loneliness. I missed my mom, my dad, and my grandparents. My friend Shawn moved back down South with her parents. I had my family, but something seemed missing. I realized that I was the matriarch of the family. I had no mentor. I wanted a surrogate mom, or something. That was when Joann came into my life.

I met Joann reading at a metaphysical store that I used to frequent before the "Church Ladies" that owned the store started talking about me behind my back. (This was the store that introduced me to reading, so I guess that I at least owe them that.) I really wasn't surprised they were rumor spreaders, they talked about everybody. You have to know that if people are talking about others, they are talking about you. Both Joann and I got sick of them eventually. That was kind of a uniting force for both of us. Nothing is worse than a bunch of "so-called" spiritually-evolved people pretending to be good humans.

Joann was only a few years younger than my mom. She had retired and was renting an apartment close to the horrible store. She had retired from the glass factory that she had worked at most of her life. I was the one who actually invited her for coffee. We hit it off immediately. We were both Sags. We became inseparable.

With my friend Joann in 2013

She told me later that she had missed an old friend of hers named Lonnie so badly, that she manifested it to me. (She got pretty close with the name Lana, didn't she?)

Joann had all kinds of talents. She also did something that I thought was kinda neat. She could read the playing card deck of 52, something I knew nothing about.

The deck of 52 had actually always been meant to be a Tarot deck. It was the original Tarot deck. That's why it correlated to the calendar: 52 cards equals 52 weeks, 4 weeks equals 4 suits, etc.

Joann knew them well. She was in her sixties when I met her. She had been reading cards for over thirty years and knew those decks in and out. But her specialty was numerology, and she taught me a lot about it. Things that I still use.

Everyone does Numerology differently. For Joann, she used the first three letters of your name to give her a snapshot about a person. The first time she read for me, I'll never forget.

"You are a creative person, aren't you? You have lots of ideas. Are you in the Arts?"

"Yes, " I smiled. "I'm an Art Teacher and artist."

"Are you a leader, or a person in charge a lot? You must be competitive, too."

I smiled again. Yes, I was competitive. Sometimes too much. "Yes, you are right."

"You thrive off of change, you like change and travel. You are a mover and a shaker."

I smiled and nodded. She got that from just my first three letters of my name. Yep, she had me pegged.

Joann taught me many things about spirituality. I only have one photo of her and I together. I loved her dearly. I knew that she was there not forever, but for just a short time. Time that I got to just enjoy having her there. She ended up with Alzheimer's, passing at a memory care facility several years later. I stopped in one day to see her. She called me Linda, but that was OK. She was close. She passed a few months after that, at the height of COVID.

Not too long ago, I got a psychic reading at a Spiritualist camp. The medium described a psychic lady who was guiding me who could read cards and do numerology. She was described as having crazy hair.

All I did was smile.

I miss you and will always love you, Joann! I hope I've done you proud! What she taught me is listed below.

Numerology: How it Works

Numerology has been around for thousands of years. It was used by the Babylonians and Egyptians. Pythagoras was said to have invented the form we know today. He said that numbers were connected to universal vibrations. There are several schools of thought on this.

Chaldean Numerology has to do with your name and the energy surrounding it. It is based on the idea of how numbers form patterns, and patterns repeat themselves. Numbers are structured and so are our lives. Time also repeats itself, much like the organization of numbers. Everything in the Universe is structured.

Kabbalah is Jewish Mysticism. I am very Kabbalistic in nature. I have been studying this for many years. It has to do with the alphabet, numerology, and related energies. I am convinced from what I read about Jesus, he knew well the aspects of Kabbalah.

Life Path

One thing you can figure out is your purpose using numerology. It's called your life path. It's the real you. It represents your overall journey. It's about your talents, hopes, and desires. It's about who you are at your core. It's what journey you are meant to follow. It's based on your birth-date.

How to Figure Your Life Path Number

Your Life Path Number is what you are trying to learn and achieve on this lifetime. By looking at the numbers, you can figure out what you are here to learn:

1. Write down your birth date, using the full year. For example; 11/19/1989.
2. Add the numbers together 1+1+1+9+1+9+8+9=39
3. You are a 3, and that is what you are trying to learn in this lifetime.

All life paths have different journeys and themes. Here are some listed below.

In Numerology, zero really doesn't exist. It is void. It is considered infinity, because there is no beginning and no end. The number reoccur from 1-9.

Number 1: You are and must be number one. You are probably a type A personality. You are a leader and a go-getter. You are unique and ambitious, one of a kind. You are a trailblazer and are assertive. You need to be mindful of being controlling, however. You are innovative. It is also related to New Beginnings.

Number 2: You are balanced, and likable. You are peaceable and seek harmony. You have an attitude of "Can't we just all get along?" You have a tendency to have quite an empathic nature. You are probably a caregiver. You probably have the rare gift of patience. People have a tendency to take advantage of your caring nature.

Number 3: Creativity is your thing. You are joyous and find joy in all creative endeavors. You are a great communicator. You express yourself clearly and effectively. You are often spontaneous and motivational to others. You also have a very intuitive ability. Sometimes, your dreaminess can keep you from accomplishing tasks, though.

Number 4: Practicality and dependability is your bag. You are conscious, organized, and thorough. You believe in hard work and its benefits. You like security and firm foundations. You are extremely honest and have high morals. You are detail oriented. You have a tendency to follow traditional norms and have trouble with things that aren't traditional, i.e., rigidity.

Number 5: This number loves freedom and movement. You are highly adaptable and love to travel. You are very adventurous. You are not afraid of transformation and may completely change your life at some point. Routine bores you. You have massive amounts of energy and tend to be restless. You are charismatic and social. You love to learn and are a risk-taker. However, you can be a little irresponsible at times.

Number 6: You are most likely a caregiver. Your home and family are the utmost importance to you. You have great empathy and compassion. You have a deep sense of community and duty to society. You have a strong affinity for beauty. You are loving spouse and parent. You are often a mentor to others. You congeniality sometimes makes you too passive.

Number 7: You are extremely spiritual. You seek higher Knowledge. You are a very deep thinker. You are introspective and a philosopher. You are analytical and intellectual. You are mystical and have psychic abilities. You are probably an introvert. You are very private. You are often your own worst enemy due to your perfectionism. You seek the higher truths in life. Sometimes, you are very anti-establishment, and some of your ideals seem otherworldly.

Number 8: You are the number of power. Your number is the infinity sign, representing the ability to manifest and produce instance karma. You are materialistic and ambitious. You are extremely powerful and have some type of authoritarian position in life. You are responsible and practical. You are determined. You are well balanced between the material and spiritual realms. You believe in justice. People who mess with you get their karma. Be careful to not be aggressive or a bully.

Number 9: You are altruistic. You are a humanitarian. You have a deep desire to make the world a better place. You are idealistic and have vision. You are creative. You are tolerant of others and are enlightened. You have a mature approach and understanding about life. You are empathic. You seek completion. Sometimes, your ego creates a thinking of being better than others.

Master Numbers
Master numbers are significant in their own right. If you notice, they are 2, 4, and 6 when added together. They have the qualities of those numbers infused into their purpose. 22 is a 4, which is half of 8, so it behaves as such.

Number 11: You are spiritually aware, intuitive, and mystical. You are visionary and inspirational. You have great empathy and compassion. You are a healer, often an emotional one. You are often too hard on yourself and critical to your own flaws. At your core, you are here to help others.

Number 22: You are a great manifester, with vision and insight. You have great power and influence. You have so much ambition and drive you sometimes lack self-care. You are responsible and well disciplined.

Number 33: This is the number of the Master Teacher. Jesus Christ is a 33. You are a visionary and truly inspiring. You are intensely spiritually aware. You are creative and may be a healer. You will create a lasting legacy of some type. You have humanitarian efforts and are nurturing and caring with an empathic flare.

Number 44: You are the king or queen of manifestation. You are the master architect. You are ambitious and determined. You have a "take no prisoners" attitude. You are leader. You are concerned about lasting achievements. You have a structured way in which you do things that is very effective. You have a sense of obligation to society or others.

Your Destiny Number

A destiny number is different than your life path. Your destiny number is more like your potential if you follow your life path. It's how you "express" yourself in this lifetime. Both Destiny and Life Paths have the same themes, but each number has certain attributes. The Destiny Number and Life Paths manifest themselves in slightly different ways.

It's not at all hard to figure out your destiny number. It's based on Chaldean Numerology. Make sure to use your full birth name as on your birth certificate, spelled the same way. This includes your middle name. Every letter corresponds to a number. Here is the chart below.

1	2	3	4	5	6	7	8	9
A	B	C	D	E	F	G	H	I
J	K	L	M	N	O	P	Q	R
S	T	U	V	W	X	Y	Z	

So, my first name Lana, would be L=3+A=1+N=5+A=1=1

I do the name thing for my middle name and last name. You will come up with one number or a master number. This number represents HOW it manifests.

Again Zero does not exist in numerology singly. It's void, or infinity.

Number 1: This destiny number represents you as a creative leader, problem solver, and self-sufficient. You are trying to lead without needing help from anyone. You are innovative and are probably creating something no one else has. It's likely this number is involved in politics, corporations, engineering, or business owners. Be carefully not to be controlling or pushy.

Number 2: This destiny number manifests itself in the area of diplomacy. You may be a Social Worker, Human Resources Director, a Project Manager, or something else that involves cooperation, likability, and harmony. You will be using empathy and love and bring it to others. Be careful not to be taken advantage of.

Number 3: The Destiny Number 3 manifests itself in some type of creativity or in a creative and communicative way. Social Skills are of the utmost importance. This number is the number of optimism and positivity. This number excels in teaching, writing, the Arts, motivational speakers, and to inspire and communicate. Stay grounded and out of the clouds.

Number 4: This destiny number is one of hard work, organization, and tradition. I think of this number as one of conformity and tradition. It has to do with details, stability, and security. It is dependable and loyal. People with this number might be housewives, traditional fathers, in the military, accountants, police officers, fireman, or work for the government. Don't try to be too rigid and unspontaneous all the time.

Number 5: This number is the number of change, adaptability, freedom, and independence. This is the number of adventurers and risk takers. This number has charisma, and loves learning. It manifests in areas such as Stock Market Traders, Tour Guides, Business Owners, politics, or someone who changes careers also a lot. This number can flit around without accomplishing their goals.

Number 6: This number has to do with service to others, and caregiving. It has empathy and caring. This number represents responsibility and reliability. This number represents harmony and balance. This number is a great negotiator and is the glue that holds working relationships and family together. This number may manifest as Social Workers, teachers, nurses, or other areas where the attitude, "Can't we all just get along" is needed. This number needs to make sure they don't become a martyr.

Number 7: This number manifests in spirituality and the wisdom of deep thinking and introspection. This is the seeker of truth and knowledge. It is highly intellectual and skeptical. It questions everything and is an idealist. It manifests in careers such as philosopher, professor, astronomer, psychic, or Reiki Healer. The meaning of life is always on their minds. This number can easily become depressed because of the horrible condition of the world.

Number 8: This number is associated with power and manifestation. This number is ambitious and driven. It has leadership qualities and financial and material success. They are practical, realistic, and are hardworking. This number needs to learn about balance of karma. This number manifests in careers like CEOs, politicians, Stock Brokers, and corporations. Care needs to be taken to prevent bullying.

Number 9: The manifestation of this number is humanitarian pursuits and development of compassion. This number practices altruism, is artistic and creative. This number is selfless and experiences deep emotional challenges. The careers in this number might be research, religion, healthcare, or caregiving. This number can sometimes develop a holier-than-thou attitude.

Master Number 11: This number is that of messenger. The person with this number might be very religious, have psychic ability, be drawn to religion, are empathetic and true visionaries. This number manifests itself in careers such as pastor, psychic, therapist or teacher. This number needs to be careful for anxiety and depression.

Master Number 22: While this number is practical, it is also a visionary. This number is considered a master builder and a responsible leader. This number has high integrity and morals. This manifests in a great work ethic and strength. The careers could be in construction, architecture, CEO, or governmental agencies. Care must be given to not become judgmental of others.

Master Number 33: This number is about unconditional love and acceptance. It is the number of Master Teachers. This number holds high amounts of spiritual awareness. Those with this number understand service to others. They are often healers. They are often martyrs. This number manifests itself as Healthcare workers, Religious teachers, and philanthropists.

Master Number 44: This number is the Master healer or manifester. This number builds on a grand scale. People who have this number are very focused. This number is practically intelligent, and yet has a desire for stability and security. This number MAKES things happen through sheer will. The number manifests in the areas of philanthropy, healthcare, governmental projects or architecture. This sign can overwork themselves into ill health.

So what you need to do is to do both of these numbers and put them together to give yourself a snapshot of yourself, or another person. So for example, a person is a Lifepath 8 and a Destiny number of 5. This person is a great manifester, who is very motivated and ambitious. As a Destiny Number of 5, they are creative and charismatic. They would probably be a great motivational speaker, coming up with new methods to teach others.

You can also figure other numbers using this system. If you add just your vowels together, that is your soul's urge and adding just consonants together, you get the "true you." Try it. It's lots of fun.

Learning the Deck of 52

I know that I've talked a lot about Tarot decks, but all of this can be applied to the deck of 52, as well as Numerology also. The cards 1-10 correspond to their rightful numerology listed above, Aces are 1, etc.

Clubs=Wands
Spades=Swords
Cups=Hearts
Pentacles=Diamonds

For me personally, my birth date coincides with the Queen of Hearts, and is also the Queen of Cups. This coincides with my Moon sign, and often appears as me in spreads. Yes, the deck of 52 is extremely accurate for those who know how to read it. There's a system referring to charts where you can find your birth date. Some call it a Destiny Chart.

Figure out your numbers and go for it! I bet you were right if you use your intuition. We usually have an idea of who we are, and if you don't have a clue, now you do!

	JAN	FEB	MAR	APR	MAY	JUN	JUL	AUG	SEP	OCT	NOV	DEC
1	K♠	J♠	9♠	7♠	5♠	3♠	A♠	Q♦	10♦	8♦	6♦	4♦
2	Q♠	10♠	8♠	6♠	4♠	2♠	K♦	J♦	9♦	7♦	5♦	3♦
3	J♠	9♠	7♠	5♠	3♠	A♠	Q♦	10♦	8♦	6♦	4♦	2♦
4	10♠	8♠	6♠	4♠	2♠	K♦	J♦	9♦	7♦	5♦	3♦	A♦
5	9♠	7♠	5♠	3♠	A♠	Q♦	10♦	8♦	6♦	4♦	2♦	K♣
6	8♠	6♠	4♠	2♠	K♦	J♦	9♦	7♦	5♦	3♦	A♦	Q♣
7	7♠	5♠	3♠	A♠	Q♦	10♦	8♦	6♦	4♦	2♦	K♣	J♣
8	6♠	4♠	2♠	K♦	J♦	9♦	7♦	5♦	3♦	A♦	Q♣	10♣
9	5♠	3♠	A♠	Q♦	10♦	8♦	6♦	4♦	2♦	K♣	J♣	9♣
10	4♠	2♠	K♦	J♦	9♦	7♦	5♦	3♦	A♦	Q♣	10♣	8♣
11	3♠	A♠	Q♦	10♦	8♦	6♦	4♦	2♦	K♣	J♣	9♣	7♣
12	2♠	K♦	J♦	9♦	7♦	5♦	3♦	A♦	Q♣	10♣	8♣	6♣
13	A♠	Q♦	10♦	8♦	6♦	4♦	2♦	K♣	J♣	9♣	7♣	5♣
14	K♦	J♦	9♦	7♦	5♦	3♦	A♦	Q♣	10♣	8♣	6♣	4♣
15	Q♦	10♦	8♦	6♦	4♦	2♦	K♣	J♣	9♣	7♣	5♣	3♣
16	J♦	9♦	7♦	5♦	3♦	A♦	Q♣	10♣	8♣	6♣	4♣	2♣
17	10♦	8♦	6♦	4♦	2♦	K♣	J♣	9♣	7♣	5♣	3♣	A♣
18	9♦	7♦	5♦	3♦	A♦	Q♣	10♣	8♣	6♣	4♣	2♣	K♥
19	8♦	6♦	4♦	2♦	K♣	J♣	9♣	7♣	5♣	3♣	A♣	Q♥
20	7♦	5♦	3♦	A♦	Q♣	10♣	8♣	6♣	4♣	2♣	K♥	J♥
21	6♦	4♦	2♦	K♣	J♣	9♣	7♣	5♣	3♣	A♣	Q♥	10♥
22	5♦	3♦	A♦	Q♣	10♣	8♣	6♣	4♣	2♣	K♥	J♥	9♥
23	4♦	2♦	K♣	J♣	9♣	7♣	5♣	3♣	A♣	Q♥	10♥	8♥
24	3♦	A♦	Q♣	10♣	8♣	6♣	4♣	2♣	K♥	J♥	9♥	7♥
25	2♦	K♣	J♣	9♣	7♣	5♣	3♣	A♣	Q♥	10♥	8♥	6♥
26	A♦	Q♣	10♣	8♣	6♣	4♣	2♣	K♥	J♥	9♥	7♥	5♥
27	K♣	J♣	9♣	7♣	5♣	3♣	A♣	Q♥	10♥	8♥	6♥	4♥
28	Q♣	10♣	8♣	6♣	4♣	2♣	K♥	J♥	9♥	7♥	5♥	3♥
29	J♣	9♣	7♣	5♣	3♣	A♣	Q♥	10♥	8♥	6♥	4♥	2
30	10♣		6♣	4♣	2♣	K♥	J♥	9♥	7♥	5♥	3♥	A♥
31	9♣		5♣		A♣		10♥	8♥		4♥		Joker

Used with Permission from Know Your Destiny Cards

When Destiny Gives You A Sucker Punch

Man, those years of teaching went by fast. I guess until you've gotten to that point, you don't really realize it. I think my soul realized it, though. I went through my mid-life change and did a few stupid things. Those that I now realize who taught me so much. In 2016, I walked out of my teaching job in Illinois. I was told later the kids cried in the halls.

Just remember, you sometimes never know how much you impact people, for good or for bad. Remember to use comforting words with ease and critical words with caution.

Now, I'm not going to, while teaching, talk about the time and the many, many episodes that could be made into a book. Like the time a kindergartner brought a dildo and handcuffs to show and tell, or the student who brought a loaded handgun to kill one of my students. If I hadn't been absent that day, and the kids split to different classrooms, we all would've been shot. There was another time one of my kids brought a very sharp machete to class in which I ripped it out of his hands and told him to quit playin'.

You just have no idea how bad some schools are. Things are often kept quiet. The harassment from other teachers was so bad, you just wouldn't believe it, either. You'd think there would be comradery in such a bad environment, but no, there was envy, jealousy, and backstabbing.

I'll never understand why women don't support each other more. I feel our culture creates this competition among women. It's something about alpha women and competition. Everyone can be in the limelight. The spotlight is big enough for everyone to shine.

I'm not sure why I was always targeted, but I was close with my students and took a personal interest in them. There was a lot of jealousy because I was liked so much by my students. It made the other teachers insanely jealous. They would passive-aggressively lash out.

Here we go again, I thought. I was being harassed, and I just decided that I was done. I often wonder why I was always being harassed, but now I realize I had allowed it by not standing up for myself. I never wanted trouble, so that left the doorway open. Now in retrospect, I had a lawsuit the whole time. It was a very valuable lesson that I learned also.

Teachers, as I stated before, are some of the nastiest co-workers on the planet. This woman, Judy, decided she didn't like me. I had been teaching for about ten years in a school I loved. I had been bullied there also by the nastiest principal that I had ever met. She literally threw my plants in the trash that sat on my windowsill, just to harass me.

2013 was one of the hardest years of my life. In the span of three months, I was being harassed by a boss that literally told me, "I want you gone." I totaled my car, my daughter had my first granddaughter and nearly died, and my other daughter nearly died of a Crohn's flair up. All in just three months. I look back, and can't believe I made it. But we are more resilient than we will ever know.

My middle daughter was with a real loser boyfriend when she found out she was pregnant. She was living with me at the time. When she gave birth, things were a mess. I predicted everything.

I predicted my granddaughter's day of birth. I told her the day and time. My daughter tried to prove me wrong. The day she delivered she had seen the doctor. She came home and said, "Well mom, you're wrong." I chalked it up to me not being one hundred percent accurate. Two hours later, the doctor called. She wanted my daughter back. She delivered on the day I said, a couple of minutes before midnight.

The birth was very hard on my daughter. Something was wrong. She was in so much pain, she couldn't move. The doctor had also nicked her ureter (the tube that allows you to move pee from your kidneys). All she did was cry. She thought she was going to die. She even willed my granddaughter to me just in case.

I knew something was wrong. I kept seeing a circle in her abdomen. We took her back to the doctor for a second time, then a third. I'll never forget that blank look on the doctor's face.

She looked at me with a blank look and said, "I really don't know what is wrong."

I calmly looked at her with a stare and said, "She has an infection under the c-section incision. It needs to be cleaned out, NOW."

How I knew this I don't know, but I was right. We found out later that her body had walled off the infection, so it looked like it wasn't there.

I thought back for a moment. My body had done the same thing. I had a severe infection while I was pregnant with that daughter in my sinuses. My body walled off the infection, and no one knew what was going on. My eldest daughter had a Crohn's attack like that. Many years later, come to find out, from a little research, this ability to wall off infection is why my family survived the Black Plague.

The doctor had my daughter in surgery within ten minutes, and I knew that I had saved her life.

At the same time my oldest daughter was in the hospital, with a severe flare up of Crohn's disease. Crohn's disease it a horrible autoimmune disease where your own body attacks your intestines. She had been through stress and had to have emergency surgery to take out about a foot of colon. They sewed her back together, but it didn't take. Her bowels and its contents were spilling into her body cavity. I watched as she got more and more withdrawn, she started turning gray, literally. And those quacks just let her sit there in the hospital. It was me that demanded more tests. It was me who they called a "bitch." It was me that also saved this daughter's life, too.

I'll never forget when she called me. I could hear the panic in her voice.

"Mom, the surgery didn't take. I'm developing sepsis. They are doing emergency surgery again."

I knew something wasn't right. I had talked to the pompous ass of a doctor and requested information when I had seen her turning gray.

He literally insulted me when I was at the hospital. He basically called me "bitch" for questioning him.

Everyone, listen to me. If the narcissistic doctor calls you names or disrespects you, question him/her anyways. I see so many people not question doctors. Remember that they are human, too. If you think he/she is wrong, question them anyways.

I was scared. I couldn't lose my baby. That is a parent's worst nightmare. I drove up to the hospital, crying the whole time. When I got there with my husband, she was not there. They had taken her for tests, but something that surprised me to this day that still resonates to this day.

When I entered the room, a little blond boy was sitting on the edge of the bed, kicking his foot. He looked amazingly similar to my husband. I was surprised.

"Who are you?" I asked.

"I'm your grandson. My name is Cameron."

I knew right then that Savannah would be OK. She was going to have a child. That meant that she would be OK. She was going to live.

After Savannah's surgery, I asked her, "By the way, what would you ever name your child if you had one?"

Savannah answered without hesitation, "I like the name Cameron." As of the writing of this book, she has not yet had him. But I am just waiting for him to come into the picture. She is pregnant as we speak with a little boy. I know it's him. I saw him playing with my mom, their great grandma. Yes, we all know our ancestors on the other side.

During this long three months, I had a so-called friend who was harassing me about being at the hospital. He said I was lying. He said he had things to do and "business was business." I should have known and cut him out of my life then. I just guess that I didn't want to believe that he was such a narcissist. He ended up later really screwing me over. He was also a misogynist and could not handle a successful, strong woman. It was always about him. He was supposed to help me with my business. We were to start one together, and repeatedly, it wouldn't go through. I backed out two times when my gut feel was to run. I'm not sure why I let him back into my life.

When things don't manifest the way you think they should, take note. The Universe was telling me NOT to get involved with this guy. I should've listened better. He ended up causing me a lot of heartache. My guides were trying to tell me. They gave me clear messages. Take note when things that happen. The Universe always has your back.

I had met him somewhere to talk business, and as I was driving back in winter, I hit black ice, and a truck pulled out in front of me on I-90. I spun out and totaled my car. Sometimes, I forget to wear my seatbelt. This time, I had made sure it was clicked. Again, my guides or maybe my soul was remembering my chart. I don't know which one. One of my other psychic friends told me I had a car accident coming.

I was head-to-toe bruised from the seatbelt, but other than that I was OK. Most people say bad things happen in threes. This was five. Just remember all of this in three months.

Remember, I was being harassed at work also by a nutcase named Judy. She sicked a supervisor on me who wanted me "gone." She came into my classroom to do a review.

It was ridiculous. She picked apart my lesson, saying that I had the wrong year on a research study. I couldn't believe it. Anything to discredit me.

She had never liked me. Several years before, she had picked on me non-stop. It took five years for her to leave me alone.

I am convinced that because of her own insecurities and low self-esteem, she picked on overweight people. I had seen the pattern. There were two other teachers she was harassing. Both also had a weight problem. Believe me when I say this to you: in the United States, obesity is the only unprotected group in this country when it comes to discrimination.

Shortly after, this Art Supervisor wanted a "fact-finding" mission and called a meeting with my principal, the Union Representative, and the bitch Judy.

I was so nervous, I spent the night before throwing up. I wasn't sure what would happen.

It's Called Karma-HA HA HA

The reason that I was targeted I still think was that it had to do with my not just my weight, but also my religious beliefs. I made it no secret that I was a medium and a psychic. Judy was Catholic. "Nuff said." Every chance she got, she tried to discredit me, telling everyone that I didn't know how to teach, and a myriad of other things, even though she had never been in my room or saw me teach. Funny that the kids all literally cried when they found out that I had left. They have the truth. Funny how many of those students, more than once, have stopped me on the street and told me what a difference I made in their lives.

This Judy piece of garbage would go to new principals about me, with little merit to back herself up. It was only about a month or so after totaling my car that we had our "meeting." She called it a "fact finding mission." I went to the meeting, deciding not to say anything. I just sat listening. There was really not much else I could do at that point. All in the span of three months.

There's No Fool Like An Old Fool

Firstly, this supervisor accused me of lying about my car accident. She asked me what kind of car I drove. I shook my head, shocked. She then accused me of lying about my children. Now, remember, my Union Rep was there, taking notes. The supervisor then told me everyone was laughing at me for making all these stories up. Um . . . OK . . .

At this time, I had a principal who knew what she was pulling. He knew this supervisor was a troublemaker, just like Judy. He, too, sat there, listening, with a somewhat shocked look on his face.

After listening to her rant for awhile, he calmly smiled and said, "I don't care how you get to work. Come on a skateboard for all I care. I don't care what happens as long as you are giving these kids an education. This meeting is over."

I knew that I had the ammo I needed. I had the Union taking notes. I had three witnesses. This was one of the first times I decided I wasn't going to take it anymore.

The next day I called the Superintendent. I demanded to talk to him. He refused. I had the Union call. He refused. So then, I had Union attorney call. BINGO! I got a call the next day. The Superintendent apologized and told me that the supervisor was getting walked out of the district after thirty-one years. It took a month or so, but when I heard she was walked out, I was screaming with joy in the halls.

Karma is always sweet, but not always swift. Karma is a plate best served cold. Just always do your best, and let God handle it.

Although the Supervisor got fired, I still had Judy harassing me. Looking back, I had a huge lawsuit. This time the Union refused to do anything. In another life, I wonder what I had ever done to her. Maybe I had done something, and this was payback from a past life. I never really found out if she directly got her karma, but many years later, I found out she got a horrible chronic disease.

In 2016, I finally decided I was done. Yes, it screwed up my pension somewhat, but I learned I didn't have to take it anymore. It was a very valuable lesson.

I took a huge pay cut, but I learned something very valuable. It was never about me and my ability to teach. It was her. It always had been. She was the one that couldn't teach. That's often how it happens.

The new school was tough, but I loved it. They thought I was one of the best teachers they ever had. This school accepted me for who I was and embraced the fact that I was a psychic. In fact, they thought it was pretty cool. It was something that I shall always hold dearly. That lesson taught me that not always is the money worth it.

If it costs you your peace, it's too expensive.

Don't Look Back, You Aren't Going that Way

There have been many other odd things that have happened, I don't even think they are odd anymore. Sometimes I even forget about them. Like the realization that we astral travel at night, visiting the otherside as well as people in this lifetime. We get better at this as we advance, and we even get better at the entrance and exit.

Do you ever feel like you are falling or have ever been frozen by fear at night where you can't talk or breathe? You are not being attacked. As I mentioned earlier, you are slamming back into your body or are leaving it too fast to astral travel. As you mature, you will realize that you can easily tell your soul to make a smooth transition coming in and out. I know now that I enter and exit through my feet. I can't remember the last time I had a bad transition.

It's all about telling your soul and aligning the physical body with the soul. We are often fragmented, separated from our souls through ignorance or fear. It's often through religious dogma that creates the fear. Your soul tries to communicate, and your ego blocks it. It's like that with dreams, too.

Dreams are a way our souls communicate, be it from messages from angels, or guides, or even a visitation from a loved one.

There are five types of dreams.

1. **Fear Dream**–This is your subconscious trying to work through the fear.
2. **Wish Dream**–This is something you want or wish for, either physically or wish to happen. Your subconscious is wanting it.
3. **Visitation**–Someone from the otherside is coming to see you, or you are going to see them. These people may just want to be around you. They may also give you messages. It could even just to tell you that they love you.
4. **Past-Life Replay**–These dreams replay past lives. Sometimes, you think that they don't make sense. You cannot remember, but your soul can. Your soul is still processing the information from that lifetime. I know I used to dream about a horrible tornado a lot growing up. My soul was trying to release trauma.
5. **Premonitions**–These are future events to come. They could be a death, a birth, or even more mundane things. Maybe our soul is trying to prepare us.

Dreams really do tell us things. Sometimes we don't understand. Sometimes we are even blocking them. We often block them because we're told it's not real or out of fear. I cannot tell you how many people tell me, "Lana, I can't remember my dreams."

First of all, get a dream journal. I sell them on Amazon (Lana's Enchanted Skye Dream Journal), but a notebook will do. Next, tell yourself to remember your dreams, and you will. Remember, you are in control. You fear and lack of belief in blocking it. Remember, too, that belief is the gateway. It's the possibility that all things are possible. That mindset allows you access to everything.

This was about the time that I started my YouTube channel and started getting orbs, angels, fairies and ectoplasm on the videos, You can see these at any time, and I invite you to watch many of my taped videos as well as live. There are thousands of instances. I also know I'm not the only intuitive out there who has this occur.

What I think these are is that they are guides and angels who bring messages to share with those who need it. I have actually slowed down the white orbs to see a simple winged being in a praying position. I think they are seraphim (tiny angels), and they give me information to share with people. I'm just not completely sure, I invite you to watch my videos and see the orbs and beings.

I've also been told when I'm live on my Social Media that there are several guides (beings, entities), who are standing behind me. Most of my followers can see a bit of a shadow and some features of people.

I do want to tell you that your guides can change throughout your life, and often do. You can also "drum up" ancestral guides by doing your family tree.

For me, my original guide was Angela. I discovered her name looking through a book on how to find your guide's name. The word "Angel" jumped out at me. Maybe the name is Angel, but it really doesn't matter. Guides really don't care what you call them.

About the time I visited Taos, I picked up two new guides: Dances in the Wind and Red Cloud. The first was an old Native shaman, and the other was a warrior. I picked up Dances in the Wind in Taos, New Mexico.

When A Guide Follows You Home Like a Stray Dog

Back in 2008, I visited one of my favorite places, Taos, New Mexico. It changed my life in more than one way. I had no idea it would be one of my strangest paranormal experiences that I've experienced in my life.

I decided I wanted to take a pastel class and visit New Mexico at the same time. I wanted to know where Georgia O'Keefe lived (She is one of my heroines). And I wanted to go by myself.

I stayed at San Geronimo Lodge. It's a beautiful, 1920s lodge with lots of history. It's also very, very haunted.

I found it interesting that the people who owned the lodge at the time would never admit it was haunted. They never answered my questions, like who was the ghost cowboy that leaned over the fondest counter, staring at me, or why did in the kitchen sound like every single dish fell, but nothing was outta place when I went into the kitchen. Or the fact that the room that I stayed in was horribly haunted. I believe it was room ten.

I found out after I left, that the room I stayed in was notoriously haunted. Many workers didn't even want to go in there.

The first night, I started hearing things. A Native American was dancing around in circles around the bed. I was still coming into my gifts, and I was terrified. This was one of the first times that I had ever been completely alone. Really alone. No husband, no kids. Maybe this is why everything was so intense. I actually think it was partially due to the fact that I was having a spiritual awakening.

The entity that appeared was old, very old. He had his hair drawn together with a string of leather down low on his back. His chest was bare, except for a breast plate made of beaded deer antler that sat in rows down his chest. He only had two feathers worked into his hair.

He danced around my bed every night. He wanted to know why I didn't get up and dance with him. I remember literally putting my pillow over my head out of fear and fatigue. On one of the last days, I remember promising him that we would get up early and go hiking if he'd let me sleep. I kid you not. I heard a huge bang, like a closing door. He left me alone to sleep. I told him he could come back when I asked and he did. We went for a walk that morning.

This was where I think I also began my interest in herbalism. He gave me recipes to this day. These recipes are ones that when I looked them up were so accurate, it led me to know for sure that it wasn't made up.

One recipe was for a sunburn. I had gotten a bad burn and needed a remedy. This is what he told me. I wrote it down:

Sunburn Remedy
1 part animal fat
1 part Prickly Pear Cactus
Rub on and leave it

And yes, I didn't realize there was Prickly Pear Cactus there, and yes, this is actually a real remedy.

I got other remedies and concoctions. This guide followed me home. He's still with me.

Things got even stranger when I left. I drove to the airport in Albuquerque. I stayed in a hotel that night because my flight was early. I was only ten to fifteen feet from my door to the car, and my keys disappeared, literally. I swear I put them on the table next to the bed. They vanished into thin air. I walked back and forth at least ten times.

No one was in the hall. I still cannot believe it to this day. I had to have the car literally towed to the rental company. No one ever found them.

That night, I kept hearing in my head clearly, "We don't want you to go." I heard it over and over and over. Yeah, "those" beings really didn't want me to leave. I never figured out what happened, but I bought a little pin from Albuquerque Airport that said, "This symbol represents the queen of lost keys." I saw it in a gift shop and laughed my ass off. How fitting.

Dances in the Wind came home with me from that trip. He has been active until about 2018. I think he's still there. He's the one who gives me info about herbs and how to use them when I am doing readings. But I have a new guide. I call him Red Cloud, but I don't think that's his real name. But like I said, guides don't care what you call them.

As for myself, I have changed main guides three times. All of my personal guides have been Native Americans. I am only 1% Native, but I feel a strong connection to the culture because of my many past lives as a Native American.

I hear lots of people say they are drawn often to a certain culture or place, and I believe it to be true. I often feel my 5th great grandmother, Minta Straighttail guides and helps me. Maybe she is my guide Angela. Who knows?

We often reincarnate on a certain continent or place because we enjoyed a certain lifetime there. I've been a Native American at least ten times, and a White settler in the 1800s at least two times, maybe three. After my past-life regression, I remembered them much better.

It's So Bizarre, It Just
Can't Be Made Up

I started really recognizing people and was often remembering places even more easily from the past. I saw so many people, some were surprising, others were laughable.

I taught with a man who, in another life, sent for me to be his mail-order-bride. I was thirteen and from Laos. I remember it clearly. In this life, he was just a co-worker. Funny how we change roles, isn't it? I don't remember my life in Asia very clearly, but I sure remember everything about where I lived here in the United States, right up to the smell of the hay in the barn where he kept me like an animal.

It was this time that I met some really true soulmates. One was Jack, and another was Eduardo. He appeared as my Veterinarian I didn't know who he really was until he handed me a pen. We touched hands, and I remembered everything. It scared the crap out of him.

I couldn't help myself. I started spewing information about past-lives. I asked him, "Where have you been?" I remembered everything: growing up together, our last name, where we lived, everything. I have verified that this place really exists and am going to go find my past-life, one of these days. We made a pact to be here now, even running into each other. I remember it from the otherside. It was meant to activate us from the otherside.

I remember clearly we had made an agreement to check on each other halfway through this life. This was now. I suddenly remembered our past lives together, even our times shared in heaven, where I made an announcement of what I am planning to do in this life.

Yeah, I was standing in front of a multitude of people, explaining what I was planning to do when I came back. (I bet those people were all of you! We are soul family!) From the group, a young, dark haired fifteen year old bounces up to me. He told me that he was coming back, too. He proceeded to tell me what he was working on. It was a lengthy, hard chart. I asked him if it was a good idea having such a hard chart. He said he could handle it.

As he was standing in front of me in this life, he proceeded to tell me about how unhappy and depressed he felt, and all I could think of was, "We told you so!"

I also think this is quite strange, but from what I can remember, he "stole" parts of my life chart that I so carefully wrote for this lifetime. He saw my chart, took some ideas from it, and made it his own. It's very interesting to see the parallel between our lives. He laughed when I told him this. " Sounds like me," he used to say. I'm not sure if the council from the otherside would allow that, but the vision sure was vivid. But often twin soul/twin flames' lives are similar. That's where things get strange. Here's how the story supposedly goes.

At least that's what most people think. Actually your twin flame can be your brother, uncle, best friend or even a parent. Seldom lyrics are they your lover. Remember you are here to do something to help the world together. It's about love.

Do not be surprised if you recognize someone, say something, and they say the same thing back. If not, look into their eyes. The eyes are the windows to the soul. They know the truth.

As for my twin soul, we occasionally run into each other. We are very aware of where we are in this life. I wish him well in the mess he calls this life.

Changing of the Guard

Now for me, my Spirit Guides have been varied. Many of my guides are Native Americans, but I have one Pot Smoking Hippy Guide who reminds me to have fun. I have at least seven personal guides, I have also seen my angel, who by-the-way is seven feet tall.

Your guides change throughout your life. I have even heard where old guides even come back into your life after an absence. And there are usually more than one Main Guide, often five or more, depending on you mission and how much help is needed. Imagine how much help this is.

How do you know? Who is there? Meditate, pray, and invoke. For angels they are here only to serve humans. All you have to do is ask. You can also communicate by asking for signs from them.

For instance, if you want some help making a decision, ask one of these guides. Say to one of them, "If I should do this, within 24 hours, send me a ladybug. If no, send me a tiger." (Time limit is important!)

Yes, they will respond. Be careful though. These answers might not appear in a traditional sense. I requested a ladybug one time, and the answer came as a picture in a color book. Just pay attention.

As these guides changed, I lost my father-in-law. He had been sick for a long time. I predicted his death.

I hate when I can predict passing. I have asked God to take this ability from me. It was just too much. But in this case, I knew almost to the day. That day, I knew something was wrong.

It was a Saturday. He had just returned home from my daughter and niece's high school graduation. They had driven up to Chicago from Florida, and now returned. I knew something was coming.

I saw it but had also heard how my father-in-law had said that he kept seeing his passed brother coming to talk to him. That's always one of the signs. The person sees people who have passed.

When I got up, I could feel this weird energy around me in the house. I even made the comment to my husband, "What is this?" It felt almost overwhelming. It felt like excitement and anxiety at the same time.

I was in the yard when my husband came to me with that "look" on his face. I knew. He didn't need to say a word. That explained the weird energy. My father-in-law was trying to get my attention. And boy did he. To be honest, I've learned a lot about the otherside from him.

He started hanging around me from the moment of his passing. He appeared in photos of me, my kids, and my sister-in-law as a turquoise orb. I have an entire video of him talking to me, running right in front of a camera, with angel flying behind him. It's on my Social Media if you look for it on YouTube Lana's Enchanted Skye

I got along with him, and yet I didn't. He was a huge misogynist and racist. (Funny thing, his great grandmother was African-American).

I realized he was this way because his self-esteem was so low. We used to tangle, and women weren't supposed to do that with him. He was the patriarch.

Anyways, I have strong convictions and opinions. This does not match our society's views of women. So my father-in-law and I clashed. And I refused to let him belittle me, be condescending, or name calling. Now you can see why we clashed. The rest of the family let him get away with it. Call me a bitch, but I didn't care anymore. I have three daughters and two granddaughters to set an example for.

And yet, after his death, he hung around with me a lot. One day, I asked him, why were you such an ass, and why now? What he told me is a priceless bit of wisdom to be shared.

"Everyone has things to learn in this life. Being an asshole was my role. If everyone always treated you right, how would you learn anything?"

He also told me about roles. Everyone picks a lifetime and plays a role, like a movie. This is not who they really are, just in this lifetime.

There are around 32 life themes that you experience in your life. This explanation will come later. For my father-in-law, his role in this lifetime was asshole. He even told me that.

Another thing that hit me is that he was not Christian. He just didn't believe any of it. And he isn't burning in the pits of hell. It reaffirmed the fact that there isn't any hell like we know it. Even though I have had Jesus come to me, I've realized there are many ways to spirituality and we are eternal. Organized religion just doesn't matter. Kindness and love matter.

There's a story somewhere in the Apocrypha (Lost Books of the Bible, taken out by the Catholic Church) where Jesus and his disciples are watching a man burn in hell. The man is screaming and gnashing his teeth. Jesus looks at his disciples and says, and I am paraphrasing, 'You know, he can get outta there any time he chooses.'

We create our own hell. We create everything. We are Godlike and can create our own reality, for good or for bad. God will not punish us because we don't believe this or that. We just need to promote love in the world. Like the phrase goes, 'Love is all you need.'

Adventures Of An
Accidental Podcast

So I started my true purpose around fifty. This is when I personally hit my North Node. I had been doing spiritual work, but it really came into focus, especially when I started my podcast. How I found that was quite interesting. I manifested it so well, it makes me laugh.

One day, I was literally looking up how to start a podcast. I was at my computer, when something in my head told me to call and ask about refinancing my house. (Yeah, those were those guides talking to me, I know, I know).

This is what was weird. I called my bank and asked to be put in touch with my normal lender. She put the call through. I got someone who I've never talked to. I found out later the call went to suburban Chicago. I later found out that it was not connected in any way to my bank branch. Not even possible to get through via phone. Someone would have had to completely hang up and make a new call. And yet, here we were, talking.

His name was Kent Jones. We started talking. He asked me about income. I told him that I worked but also ran a business. He asked me what kind. I stuttered.

At this time, I knew that many people give me very negative reactions when I tell them that I'm a medium.

"Well," I said, "I do counseling work."

" Oh, really? He seemed interested. "What kind?"

I hesitated and figured I might as well out myself.

"I'm a psychic and a medium."

Dead silence for a moment.

"You know, I've been looking for someone like you for a while. I own a podcast station. How'd you like your own show?"

That started a long relationship between Kent and I. We worked well together. There was a good chemistry between us. I met the other owner, Pete. He was a great guy, but Kent and I had a little better chemistry. 216thenet became my home even though we no longer collaborate. I still love those guys, as well as the others who would follow.

The Haunted Station

Of course as a spiritual type of station, with positivity and spirituality as it's focus, there would be odd occurrences. Besides, I seem to attract them.

The podcast station building was owned by a family. The oldest member had passed away. I think that was the older guy who kinda "did" things in the studio. Kent often wondered if it had been a former station owner. Kent and Pete had acknowledged it several times before I even came into the picture.

He likes to play pranks. He'd turn things on and off. He'd appear as shadows in photos. While I was doing a podcast one day, he appeared as an orb, streaking through the middle of the room.

"Boy, you're haunted," I mentioned one day to Kent.

"Yeah, we thought so," Kent commented. He elaborated about who he thought he was. I described the guy I could see. We both agreed that it was the former owner.

Several months later Kent told me an odd story. The entity must've been haunting the whole building. He also told me that one of the workers had just died suddenly. Either way, things were being "done" in the building. Kent proceeded to tell me that one day he could hear a ruckus on the first floor. A woman was walking around, and very loudly telling a spirit to leave. He told me that it sounded like a house clearing, only she was walking and screaming at the entity. (Like that is going to work!) Anyways, things seemed to calm down.

I cannot always see the people haunting a place, sometimes I feel them. Usually, when I do see them, it's in my third eye. I can walk into a place and tell it's haunted and what they look like. I have been hired to clear out many houses. I usually find that these are people who have not crossed, but are "stuck." Saying a prayer to Archangel Michael usually does the trick.

I also think sometimes that a haunting is created as an overlay of time. It's kinda like a tape stuck on replay in time. It's basically a time warp. I also firmly believe that some people can visit places much like astral travel and can visit places they are merely thinking of. These people are alive. They are doing a form of teleportation. Hauntings seem to come in many forms, not just the dearly departed.

I would like to take this opportunity to tell you a little bit about hauntings. I would say that about 70% of hauntings aren't really hauntings. They are balls of energy that "bounce" around in your houses. These "balls" of energy are created from negative emotions: violence, yelling, anger and so forth. I have cleared many, many houses with this negative energy that seems to create a dark depressing, almost suffocating feeling.

Cleansing Your Space

Yes, you can cleanse your space and need to do this often. Any negative thoughts, feelings or energy can "hang around." All you need to do is use a little sage, lighting it, and touching every corner of every room. You can also let sunshine in, open windows for fresh air, or even do something you love. I always invoke Michael the Archangel to protect and cleanse my space. I did at the podcast station, and it seemed to clear.

That Nasty Word COVID

I can guarantee that within a few years, we will try to forget that nasty pandemic of COVID, like our ancestors did with the Spanish Flu. It was a horrible time. I lost more than eight friends, family, and co-workers. One of them was Pete, our Podcast owner and producer.

Pete was a great guy. He was very devoted to his station. He was a quirky guy, who had several haunted dolls that he talked to and that would give him information. Even as a psychic and medium, it freaked me out a little.

Speaking about haunted dolls, yes, this happens. Spirits seem to use them to communicate. Why? They resemble humans with bodies. I am in full belief that he was communicating with those dolls. I personally won't do that. You could get some very negative entities who have not yet crossed who could wreak a lot of havoc.

It was Thanksgiving when we found out Pete had COVID. He hadn't had his vaccine and didn't want one. He went into the hospital on that Wednesday. I saw him running around, out of his body. I knew he wasn't going to make it.

When I first started doing mediumship, I could see clearly when people and how people died. I scared the shit out of me. I asked God to remove it, and he did, for awhile.. I can now see when people pass who we know are going to pass. They may tell me how they passed without the gruesome details. I see the person hopping out of the body and know they will pass. For some reason, I'm good with numbers and time frames.

I told Kent about Pete, and I knew he didn't believe me. He called later that week to give me the bad news. I hate when I am right sometimes.

Weird things started happening again at the podcast station. I saw things move around. Lots of playing with the electronics was going on. Pete has communicated with me, letting me give messages to Kent and Pete's family. Yes Pete, we know you are there, and we will never forget you!

Definition of Retirement: When You Stop Living at Work and You Work at Living

O ur soul knows everything. Ever experience déjà vu? That's your soul pinpointing things you planned before you came to let you know you are on the right track. For me, I knew that my time teaching in the public schools had come to an end.

I don't know why I did what I did, but I decided that I was done teaching after thirty-one years. That year, I literally decided that I just couldn't do it anymore. I was scared to death. How would I make ends meet? I couldn't retire yet, I had at least five more years to go. How could I make ends meet?

I made a calendar on my whiteboard at school and started marking the days. I had no idea what I was going to do. Providence smacked me in the face.

Around November of that year, one of my friends casually mentioned retirement to me.

"So, aren't you eligible to retire yet? You can retire at fifty-five."

"No, I can't," I sighed. "I'm not Tier One." Tier One were the people who got to retire at fifty-five. The lovely government raised the people beneath me to sixty. I thought I was part of the second tier.

"That makes no sense," he said. "I'm younger than you, and I'm Tier One. Maybe you better check."

I called that night to the State of Illinois Retirement System. I found out in fact, I was indeed a Tier One. I cried for about an hour out of pure joy. I retired officially on January 21st, 2022, at the end of the semester. My principal was so shocked. She didn't know what to say.

There was no pomp or circumstance, no parties, my husband didn't even take me out to dinner. After thirty-one years, I was done. I missed the students horribly at first, but I knew there was something more for me around the corner.

My soul knew what I had planned. I was simply living in my North Node. I started my North Node around 2018 when I started doing predictions in public and created seven Social Medias. My North Node, as I stated before, is Taurus. I am here to learn how to make money spiritually, live a comfortable and well grounded life, while still helping people. That is my purpose, and when you are truly in your purpose, the contentment that you feel is truly amazing.

The Cauldron Calling the Kettle Black

Anyone who knows me, knows I'm a bundle of energy. I simply don't sit around much. I love tons of exercise, and I need my mind constantly stimulated. I seldom have nothing to do; my hobbies keep me constantly busy. I seldom get really depressed but am able to pull myself out of the doldrums. Everything I do is fast; from paintings in art class to direction following. I'm always two steps ahead of the person talking to me.

As I said before, I was a diagnostician. I identified ADHD, autism, Learning Disorders, and Behavioral issues. I did this for two years. In those two years, I never dreamed what I would find out.

After retirement, I decided to get weight loss surgery. It was a compilation of tons of appointments, including a therapist for proof of mental stability in order to go through with the surgery.

I passed the requirements with flying colors. It was interesting though, that she made some observations about me.

"So, what percentage of things you start, but don't finish?" she asked.

"Um maybe, 30-40%. I just have to concentrate."

"Do you talk quite a bit, especially when you've been triggered?" She stared at me.

"Yes, I used to get in trouble in school for talking too much."

The therapist nodded her head. "I believe you may have a form of ADHD. It's different for women, you know."

Yes, I knew. I have no idea why it didn't occur to me before. I always thought I was just high energy. It makes sense now. When I really thought about it, all of my problems that I had were due to my high energy, sometimes blurting out things or the intensity that I often expressed. I'm really not depressed, just that I go and go and go. I blame it a little on my Sagittarius for placement, but active people are no surprise to my family.

Just remember that women are harder to diagnose than men, because we compensate better. For me, school was extremely easy, I finished my work easily and was not distracted. For many women, we have other characteristics like chattiness, impulsiveness, or disorganization. I really had none of these growing up, except for the chattiness, extreme bluntness, and a classroom desk that looked like a junk heap. I was fifty-seven when I was diagnosed. I'm not on meds, but I am more conscientious of making sure everything is done, take a little time to organize better, and have learned when to keep my mouth shut. Not everyone needs to be on meds.

Messages From Jesus

It happened in September of the year 2022 when I retired. There was a full lunar eclipse. I wake up a lot at night and often write my many international predictions. This night was different. I woke up and in front of me was a man. The only way I could describe him is that he looked like Jesus in all the pictures.

"Oh my gosh, it's Jesus," I remembered saying in my head. "Is this Jesus? Jesus, it's you right."

I have NEVER felt the way he made me feel, before or since. I felt like a warm teddy bear hugging me with the most love I've ever felt in my life. I was so excited, I was bursting at the seams.

Jesus just laughed at me. He has a great sense of humor.

I was amazed to see Jesus. I had always thought of myself as more Buddhist, like I said earlier. He said he needed to give me messages. I found the messages comforting and surprising at the same time. I will paraphrase what he said to me.

1. What I am doing as a medium and psychic is not wrong. He knows that I've had doubts as to whether what I am doing is evil. I have helped and healed so many people. I need to keep doing what I am doing.

2. He told me that it doesn't matter how he appeared. If I were Buddhist, Buddha would appear; and if I were Muslim, it would've been Muhammad. There are many ways to God. As long as it is about love, that is all that matters.

3. I asked why he chose me, and he said, "You are getting to the masses. I am appearing to many people right now." He also mentioned that I am not the only one that he is appearing to.

4. Jesus is on the planet, and he is working. He is tired of people doing evil in his name and the name of Christianity. Help the sick, help the poor. Love your enemies. That's where I am.

5. Jesus doesn't care if you are gay, or if you've had an abortion. He does care about who is on the planet, and how to love and help them.

6. The end times are not what you think (I do not know what he means by this, but he didn't elaborate). I think he may mean that the Bible depiction is not accurate.

7. He also told me that at my core, I am a writer. I need to write, so here I am.

8. Everything you say and do should come from a place of love. That's the only way to help the planet.

This is the photo I get when Jesus came to me in September 2022, during the lunar eclipse

I found all of this intriguing. So since then, I've been trying to spread his message. He has come a little to me since, but for some reason, he tried to make significant contact with me during full lunar eclipses. He appeared again in September of 2024, only with a much different message. He called me out.

I went to Sedona in September of 2024 for a retreat I was hosting. While I was sleeping there, I saw Jesus, but his back was to me. I told one of my friends that I didn't know why. I soon found out.

A few days later on the actual eclipse date, Jesus came to me again, this time in the morning. I asked why he turned his back to me.

Jesus told me, "Because you turned your back on me."

I was confused. I've been trying to get your message out.

"You're not doing it like I told you. I told you to tell everybody, regardless of religious or political affiliation. You are not following my directions."

It took me a moment to process this. Yes, I had been blocking right wingers who were trolling me.

"What am I supposed to do? I asked "They are tormenting me. They are making me miserable."

"Well, look at what they did to me. What you are doing is not love. Show love to those who are persecuting you. Love is all that matters."

He was right. I needed to quit removing those who didn't think or feel like I did. It's been hard since, but I am learning to try to ignore those people. I just keep telling people that Jesus is here, working to bring love.

Some of my followers have commented on this recently that we shouldn't have to be abused, either. We should separate ourselves from negativity. You see, what I was doing was not promoting love, but hate: my beliefs are right, yours are wrong. I was creating derisiveness, not acceptance. I need to love them, and let my opinions go. Trust me, I am still working on this! Jesus has been regularly appearing to me since all of this. He has been a messenger, and warns me of things to come, as you will see later.

Jesus also gave me a warning yet to come. He said there will be another disease coming. One that has been man made. It will target everyone over forty. If we stay vigilant, we can avoid it. It scared me because he showed me in the hospital. It is a type of respiratory, much like COVID (but I don't think that is it). I am not perfect, but I know think that there were two messages. I recently ended up in the hospital with my Gall Bladder out. I think who gave me two messages. I try my best to decipher things, but I am not perfect. He told me that I needed to be here on the planet, so be watchful.

This is why I'm telling you. Be careful and vigilant, and we can avoid it. I do not when it is coming but believe it from now until 2040. Be kind, show love, and try to do the best we can. Ignore negativity when possible and take care of your bodies. Ignore negativity and people with low vibrations.

People have their own paths and be vigilant.

A Life Changing Event?

I needed a trip. I felt that I needed it. I had seen a class about bending spoons with your mind on Social Media. I decided that I would take a class.

I had a feeling that I could do this. Several times when I was with my daughters ghost hunting, I had actually charged a battery. Granted it was only for a few seconds, but it still worked. I was simply using pinpointed Reiki Energy. I wanted to try to bend spoons.

I mentioned it to a few followers on my Social Media.

"I wanna come, too!" I heard a few people ask.

I decided to make it into a last minute retreat. I booked a house in Oak Creek, outside of Sedona, Arizona. I had seven people meeting me there, mostly people driving from California. I never thought about it, but I was warned by a physic friend that the trip would change my life. It did. It changed us all.

If You Could Only See What's Really Up There in the Sky

I did some research, and came up with an itinerary. I decided to connect with someone who taught everyone how to bend spoons like Yuri Geller, go UFO watching, and I taught a class of psychometry (the Art of Reading Objects).

I connected to a woman who took us out to the desert at night, using night vision goggles. I cannot tell you how much stuff we cannot see with the naked eye! Yes, those spacecraft are real! They come and go constantly. You also won't believe how many falling stars come to Earth each night. It's amazing.

I will say one thing about the experience that I know to be true. If the government is creating these aircrafts that we saw, their ability is so advanced, it would blow our minds. We saw things zooming across the sky like I've never seen. Sometimes in formations, sometimes not. They kind of looked triangular. There is intelligent life beyond ours, and the government knows about the technology. There is no doubt.

I predicted we would have contact, and the government would admit it in 2021. All I said is what I was told by my guides. There would be "contact." Funny that phrase is used widely now, but back in 2021, people literally laughed at me.

I recently also found a prediction in some of my old notes. It simply says:

"The answer to climate crises and everything wrong on this planet can be found in the ocean."

I thought it was strange when I wrote that, but now I understand. The government has told us that aliens live in the oceans. It makes total sense. The aliens are trying to help us.

We as humans are learning more about it everyday. I truly believe the aliens have been here for thousands of years and are mostly harmless entities who wish the best for us. I heard that entities of other worlds are not allowed to interfere with our evolution. However, I think they may intercede to keep us from blowing up the planet. Let's hope the latter is right.

My Tribe

On my retreat, I found my tribe. I finally felt like the real me. I felt like I totally belonged, something I had never felt. I urge everyone to find their "tribe," either that or create their own group. There is a calmness that my soul has not felt in a long, long time. These are like minded individuals, who all have a common goal with you. People at my retreats were definitely vibrating at the same frequency.

Did My Mind Bend the Spoon, or My Spoon Bent My Mind?

We took several classes, and one of them was spoon bending. This is where you concentrate on the spoon, and using energy, make the spoon bend.

My followers and I took a spoon bending class. I had this funny feeling that I could do it. I had never tried it before, but I did understand energy and knew that I could recharge batteries slightly. For some reason, I just knew I could. We started the class.

All seven of us started with spoons, and each of us bent them easily. We literally rolled, bent, and even broke them in half in some cases. Then we tried to do it with just our minds.

I was listening to the instructor, just holding my spoon by the end of it, and as I was listening, the spoon bent, nearly in half, right in front of everybody. I was as amazed as everyone in the room. Yes, it changed my life. All I could keep thinking was, "GEEZ, if I can do this, what can't I do?" Yep, life changing.

I urge all of you to take a retreat like this sometime. You don't have to go with me. Find someone who you connect with and go for it. Trust me, you will never be the same.

My Predicting Weather is Great:
My Crystal Ball Must be a Snow Globe

I started doing predictions around 2016. Looking back, I had predicted Roe Versus Wade being overturned. I have predicted a lot.

It started after my Social Media on my podcast. I started doing predictions once or twice per year. I also noticed that I forget some of my predictions because I just blurt them out in my lives. I'll never forget one time I recently made a comment to a follower who was concerned about the New Madrid fault.

I literally said, "Nah, don't be worried about that yet. I'd be more concerned about Yellowstone." Two days later, there was a small eruption in Yellowstone.

I don't remember saying many of my predictions. I don't know why, but I believe that I am channeling the information. I'm thankful for my "tribe" of followers who have helped me keep track. Many people send me confirmation of my predictions when the occur in real time.

It's interesting about my predictions. The things that I care about most seem to be my predictions that I mention the most often. One thing is hurricanes. So far, I have not missed a place that they have hit. At least since 2024, every single place that I've said would have one has hit there. The one thing that I did miss was that in 2022, I predicted there would be two hurricanes to Florida and the Carolinas, and it was one hurricane hitting twice.

My rate is not as high when predicting elections. I have predicted the most elections with a 78-84% accuracy rate. I admit, I felt Kamala Harris would win in our election, but I was told my own state of Wisconsin would go Red, and she would struggle with the Electoral College. I said this at least three to five times before the election. My guides actually kept screaming to me that the other one would win, but the energy was so heavy, I still felt she'd pull it off.

I believe I was wrong, but yet really, I feel like things have been manipulated. Also, things have been cloaked. As I write this, I am leaving it up to you to decide what you believe, but I will tell you that

I feel that I am not wrong. Many, many people in my profession said the same thing.

I took a lot of brunt for it. People told me that I was a charlatan, a fake and didn't know what I was doing, even though I have over 200 correct predictions. I went through a lot of self doubt and depression. I soon realized that these people were of evil intent, and that they were trying to bring down my vibration. It is myself as a light worker that finally saw through this and allowed them to feel anyway they wanted. They can follow me or not. That's fine with me. I am not perfect. I am a messenger.

What I believe is that since I live mostly in 4D, I do not see negativity such as lying, cheating, or stealing. I see outcomes, but when they have been changed, I only see outcomes overall.

I still say there are great things coming to the United States and to the world. We have to go through the bad stuff first.

I was doing a reading not too long ago, and a client's grandmother came through and said, "True peace is coming." That's all she'd say.

Yes, I understood this. I'm not sure how we get there from here yet. We have to keep our vibrations as high as possible to make it to the finish line. As the aliens said, everything on this planet is about time and gravity.

Time frames can be hard to predict. Time is so hard to predict on the other side! My overall prediction rate so far is 97%. How do I know my accuracy rate? Because there are people definitely trying to prove me wrong! These are the people figuring out my accuracy rates. Yes, I am being watched in more ways than one.

Nothing Starts With An N and Ends With a G

My podcast host and producer Kent has taken it upon himself to prove me wrong. He has been writing down predictions since I started, then crossing them out as they come true. This is why I know the percentage of correct predictions. He and a few people create a ratio of how many right to how many wrong. It's between 94-97% percent.

I'm not sure why or how I got this information. I believe that I am given it to inform and warn. Jesus has given information to me. So have guides. I know I've missed some. I am not perfect. I believe really big predictions I usually get right. I sometimes miss details.

Since we are now in the Age of Aquarius, I would like to take this chance to tell you a few predictions that I know will happen. Many of my predictions are about the United States, since I live there.

Most of my predictions are currently posted on my website, www.enchantedskye.com.

I am probably going to do a book of predictions, but here are a few huge predictions that I have been predicting since 2019.

1. Amending of the U.S. Constitution to include The Human Rights amendment to include Healthcare and fresh water and food as a basic human right.
2. Amendment to the U.S. Constitution to include the Equal Rights Amendment (already happened in January 2025).
3. Unbelievable strides in medicine and healthcare in 2024-2040. We will have machines that we put our hands into, bring them out, and cuts are healed!
4. Restructuring of the banking and financial system globally within the next years of 2024-2040. The dollar bill will be worthless. Could be going to cryptocurrency.
5. More local farming globally.
6. Increase of people in the United States moving to the Great Lakes by 2040.
7. Decrease in global population to 5.6 billion (Not sure if this is by War or Famine or Climate Change. I do not see the reason yet).
8. Massive rebirth and acceptance of the Native Culture in The United States.
9. Complete collapse and reforming of the United States, even the possible renaming of it. Something like the Republic

Federation of the United States of America. I think this might be by 2040 but not sure of time frames.

10. Hunger in the United States as we learn to depend upon ourselves personally (Grow your own food!).

11. ONE WORLD GOVERNMENT.

12. Full alien contact.

13. San Andres Fault shift.

14. Hover cars, much like hover boards.

15. Massive reduction in organized religion.

16. Massive reduction in things like drugs and sex rings, quite a few will be shocking, with many Hollywood people involved (I know who, I have given hints).

17. Massive reduction in pesticides, chemicals and other garbage in our food.

18. NATO and Canada will help the United States with election fraud. This is worldwide fraud. It will band us together.

I have hundreds of predictions. These are more big ones. What I see is a kinder, gentler world coming where love will reign. Remember, we are collectively raising the vibration of the planet.

Dieting is Not a Piece of Cake

In 2020, I had my Lapband removed. Lapbands are a form of gastric by-pass where a band is out around your stomach to help you lose weight. It wasn't working. I had lost no weight. I had it for more than ten years. The only good thing is that it kept me from gaining anymore. The pain became excruciating every time I ate. I tried to repeatedly tell my doctors that's what was wrong with me.

They wouldn't listen. "You just eat too much." I knew better. I only ate on an average eight hundred calories per day. I even kept track. Yes, eight hundred calories. I still couldn't get it off. If I increased it, I'd gain.

I made my decision finally in 2021 that I couldn't take this anymore. I was going to get weight loss surgery. It took me a lot of pulling strings with my insurance, after waiting and jumping through all of the hoops, I got surgery in January 2024.

The weight loss has not come off quickly, but I have noticed that I have changed my metabolism. It moves at a much faster rate. I didn't lose all of my weight but enough to keep me happy. At first, it was really hard. I went two weeks without eating solid food. But I proved to myself that I could do it. If I could do that, I could do anything.

Since I'm older, it has come off very slowly. That's OK though, at least it's coming off. As of right now, I am at a plateau of losing ninety pounds. The weight loss surgery for me has now been a toss up. While I lost weight, the surgery gave me vitamin deficiencies that I never had before and need to be watched carefully. Removing my gall bladder changed my metabolism, and again, more weight came off.

I have Hashimoto's Disease. It's an autoimmune that attacks your thyroid gland. However, my thyroid gland says it's working. I know it's not working properly. It runs in my family.

I found out that my daughter already had a goiter (That's a nodule on your thyroid). She was told she had Hashimoto's. She told me that I should be checked.

When I asked to be checked, the doctor said there was no reason. I insisted. Finally, they checked the antibody levels. My levels were 350 times above normal. Finally, I had an answer to my weight gain. I am not currently on any meds, but for me diet and exercise help tremendously. I just need to keep close tabs on it. After surgery, my antibodies went down tremendously.

I was told that this surgery would change my mindset and it has. I have healed my inner child. The one that the kids made fun of. The one that teachers and co-workers picked on. The teenager who was unnoticed and silenced.

Am I really thin yet? No, but it gives me hope. Hope is the most important thing you'll ever be given. When there is hope, there is positivity.

If you are having a hard time with weight loss, I suggest looking into doing something drastic, like myself. Some people decide not to do this, that's OK also. I just know that this surgery has healed more than my physical body. It has healed my soul.

I have healed from the outside in. I have no regrets, and my health is even better than before. Even with my vitamin problems, it's still better. It's a form of Spiritual Awakening. I have recently come into my own. The future, from what I can see, looks bright. Will I always keep all this weight off? I have heard you gain some of it back when your body adjusts, so I probably will. I have increased my exercise dramatically, so that may help.

In April 2025, I suddenly started having pains on my right side. I had been having pain off and on for years. I had tests, but I was told nothing was wrong. That day in April, the doctors finally did a CAT scan. It was infected with tons of Gall Stones. It came out. I have never felt better. Was this the source of my lack of weight loss? Seems to be true. Please pay attention to this in your own life. If your weightless stalls, there is probably an underlying reason.

It finally makes Sense

I never gave a lot of thought to the alien thing. I started reading a little about it, wondering if it were real. Well, duh. After watching the skies and what I saw in Sedona, there was no way that there couldn't be aliens. I also got the impression that there were more than one kind here, too, when I was watching. It particularly hit home realizing that we couldn't usually see them with the naked eye. I saw many different types of spacecraft; some triangles, some round. There had to be more than one type of beings.

In 2023, the mention that the government admitted that extraterrestrials are real, put my mind more in that state. I started reading about close encounters and opened up my mind.

Telling us about them and listening to others who could channel messages from other beings got me wondering more and more about this subject.

It wasn't until a follower asked me a question that seemed to rock me to my core.

"So, are you a Pleaidian Starseed?" she asked one day.

I didn't say anything back to her on the phone.

"You know, you fit the bill."

"Hmmm," I said. "I never really thought about it."

"Are we supposed to have an invasion? Why don't you study this and see what you get?"

If only I had an idea what rabbit hole this was going to take me down!

That evening, I decided to ask myself if I could get any information, and I lied down. I didn't know what to expect, but since I got most of my channeling at night, I kept an open mind. Around 1:30 a.m., I woke up and began to write. And write. And write.

First, I began to question myself. Usually, I can see the entity that is talking to me. I couldn't see anyone this time. It's like they were communicating telepathically. The voice seemed male, but I wasn't so sure. I actually wondered if I was making it up in my head. The entity assured me this was real.

I heard the word Pleiadians, and another word that sounded like Arturus. I found out later it was Arturians. Yes, maybe I could channel these beings.

I was awake for awhile and wrote enough to make my arm sore. I shared some of the information on my podcast. These beings were loving and wanted the best for mankind. It occurred to me that if these beings have been here this whole time, they would not be scary or dangerous.

These are some of the things that I was told when I channeled them. There have been many battles.

- The Pleaidians are not happy with how humans are being treated in the United States and other governments.

- We are in a battle for the embetterment of our people.

- We will take over with kindness.

- Everyone will be fed, and everyone will be clothed.

- Everyone will experience happiness and treated fairly.

- This was an experiment that you have failed through your greed.

- Your money means nothing to us.

- Society shall crumble.

- A kinder, gentler and loving world is coming.

- There will be no leader. It will be collective.

- We don't want death and destruction, but you have created it. It will come to offset the evils that you've created.

- The true leaders are those like me who lead people to true happiness.

- You do not need material things. Mother Earth and your fellow man have everything you need.

- Things are speeding up.

- We have been watching. You may not see us with the naked eye.

- Pay attention to the animals. They know everything.

- There is a huge uprising coming, one of kindness and concern for others.

- Those who are materialistic and greedy will fight this change, but to no avail.

- Eyes will be pulled open.

- Greed is the reason for all of this.

- We are here to free our people and show what true freedom from slavery is. You have been a slave to the system. A system of greed, and non-love and avarice. There shall be peace.

- Those who fight back do not want to give up their greedy, privileged ways.

- A new way of existence is coming.

- We find your elections humorous. They have been fixed by those of power and greed. You never needed them.

- Soon, you will see what real power is. We will be living in pods of people, interacting, sharing and learning.

- It's time to put down the weapons.

- Peace, true peace. No worries, no fear, no anger, no disappointment.

- Look at the animals, they are already there.

- You can cure your own diseases. So can you. The knowledge has always been there, but greed and evil have taken over.

- You are like us, coming from the same Source. We are above materialism. No one tells us what to do. We already know what is needed. So do you, you have just forgotten.

- You have been brainwashed by those who wish to control you through materialism.

- Until all hate, jealousy, avarice, pettiness, resentment, greed is gone, then you will know peace.

I got this on the first night. I literally felt my soul lift out of my body. That's how I knew what I was writing was real. Maybe Source let that happen to help me understand. I didn't even remember what I had written the next morning.

Reading it put me in deep thought. Why me? I truly thought I'd get nothing. Here was information that was truly profound.

I told my friend. She told me to see what I got the next night. I got even more.

Do not be afraid. We have learned to manipulate time and space.

We seem invisible, but we are here.

Look to the stars for the answers on how to live.

We can help you fix your health by manipulating time and gravity. Time is extremely easy to manipulate. That's how we got here. You will live ten times longer when you realize you can manipulate these things.

Yes, we helped build the pyramids. They have been built on lay lines. It helps balance the Earth to keep its rotation balanced.

We do not sleep like you do. Your need for sleep has to do with gravity and the pull of the Earth. This is what causes aging and digestion issues. Worrying also causes aging.

The government has way too much to do with your everyday lives.

We will teach you how to manifest everything so you do not need to worry. Your imagination is so powerful.

We have been here for thousands of years. We have given you technology, but you have destroyed yourselves with it.

Atlantis and Lemuria are real. They were more advanced than you are now. You have destroyed yourselves, but we feel you have evolved again enough to handle us.

Religions will crumble. They are not needed. The Source is within you. Jesus existed and understood these laws.

A one World government is coming, but not a government at the same time.

Do not be scared. It is an exciting time as we become the beings we are meant to be.

We are talking to many of you across the globe. Religious people will cling to their beliefs and bring war and famine. They will be stopped.

Weather anomalies will stop. Yes, these can occasionally be manipulated. There is no need or want if you love and respect the Earth.

Very advanced technology is coming to you soon.

Everything I say you know within your DNA. It's locked in there.

Meditation is the closest you can get to our way of thinking and our minds.

We will show you soon how to manifest your needs and desires.

There is a great awakening. Even the animals know. We will fight back.

You have God, but do not listen to what he says.

I finally stopped writing after about two hours of being shaken out of bed. I couldn't understand why. And as I sat there thinking, I looked up some things about Pleiadians and Arcturians. As clear as a bell, I heard: "You are also Lemurian."

"I am? What does "also" Mean?"

After all this time, it suddenly occurred to me. I sat up in bed. Could it be that maybe I was those things? Was this why I could hear their messages so clearly?

Yes, I've been called a light worker and a starseed. Was I Pleiadians AND Arcturian? Did I also live in Lemuria? Was this in all my lifetimes? Why am I realizing this now?

This all shook me to my core. I suddenly began to realize that in this Age of Aquarius, we are all have had amnesia and remembering who we are all collectively.

It made so much sense now; never feeling like I felt it, people were always afraid of my power. People saying and doing mean things to me for no reason. They all sensed that I was different. I've never really fit in, and now I know why. I am a Pleiadian and Arcturian Starseed. I am both, and I at one time lived in Lemuria.

WHY ARE ALIENS ALWAYS CALM? BECAUSE THEY HAVE STELLAR PATIENCE

All of this was going on, and I didn't realize who I was talking to. I just didn't understand. I just knew I was getting downloads. So one day, I asked to see who I was talking to. And I got it . . .

First, he gave me this long name, which I shortened to Mark. I originally said Mack, and he corrected me. Then he showed himself to me.

He was a very pleasant color of minty blue-green. He had a large head, pale skin, thick white hair and a small mouth with very straight, white teeth. I was unnerved to say the least.

What he said next, really hit me like a ton of bricks. He said to me mentally.

"You've seen me before."

It took me a minute, and then I realized it before. Yes, I have seen him. I caught him in a photo.

When I was in Sedona, on Rachel's Knoll, a well known vortex, I caught a picture of some very weird "things" in the sunlight, in front of a tree. I didn't know what to think when I looked at the picture. Everyone at the retreat couldn't believe it either. The picture looked like a being in the middle, with another person, and maybe eyes. (I later determined that the "eyes" were actually the tops of spaceships.)

He is Pleiadian, and this fits the bill. The Pleiadians that visit and reside in Sedona are called Essassanis. They have chosen this part of the planet because it conducts electricity so well, but there are many other places, especially near water.

Everything that I described these people to be are what I saw. The picture proves it. Supposedly the outfit they wear is that minty color that I saw. He acts for me as a sort of guide. He tells me not to fear what is to come.

 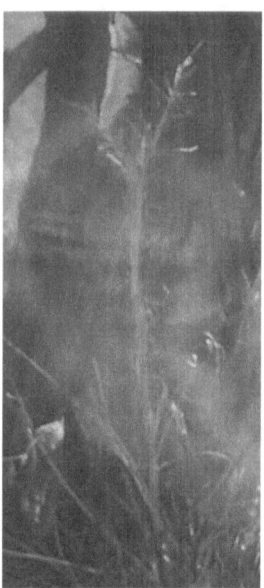

This is the Sedona Photo with the aliens in it.
The 2nd photo is the blown up version.

I asked him if he has been with me since the trip to Sedona. He told me no, that he has been here on and off with me for awhile. He is helping me with my predictions. He says that he's not with me all the time but comes through when I ask.

Recently, in January of 2025, I saw something in the sky. It was what we saw in Sedona, but much closer. It went right over my house. It was triangular, with two red lights and one white light. It had a beam that went down at an angle to the ground. It was only a couple hundred feet in the air. It was headed towards Milwaukee. Within a half hour, everyone was taking pictures of it, saying it was a drone or UFO.

I asked Mark if that was him. He said "no." But it was the start. He said I'd see more soon.

He said he'd maybe make another appearance to me. Oh, and did I forget to tell you, he has pointed ears?

Living in 4-5D

S o the farther along I get, the more paranormal, metaphysical things and vision seem to happen. I believe because we are entering the great time of manifestation and direct contact with our stellar friends. People are evolving. It's that simple.

At this present time, some unevolved people are making fun of those who are not "woke." These people are living in 3D: hate, fear, and other negative emotions. They are the ones who are just surviving. Bringing down the vibration of the Earth. These are the people who will be left behind as we ascend into higher consciousness. I believe these people will not even be able to see the other beings, until their vibration has increased.

I live in 4D most of the time. The otherside is 4D. It is a state of being where manifestation and love rule. But we need to be closer to Christ-consciousness, which is 5D. It is constant love. As humans, this is hard, but we are trying. Don't be upset if you lose it on a person who cuts you off in traffic or bullies you. You will not always be living in 5D. The difference is that you are trying. No one can ask for more. I have lots more information on this at a later date.

Yes, Manifest!

As we go from 3D to 5D, manifestation will get easier as we learn how to manipulate things around us. I can prove that you can.

If you are having trouble, start with little things: an ice cream cone, a penny, something small. Don't wish for a million dollars by the next day. You have to let things happen and occur within a reasonable time frame. Here are some rules;

1. The goal needs to be realistic. Asking for one million dollars by tomorrow is a little far-fetched. Making a million dollars in two years or four years is manageable.
2. The goal needs to be attainable. Same as above.
3. Set a time frame. Set a week, a month, a year. I put it on my wish board to remind me.
4. Be specific. Being vague can cause chaos in the Universe.

So for example, this is how I got this book published. I made a wish, set my intentions, was made specific and timely.

I want 8888.88 given to me by the end of January, 2025.

I want my book published and in my hands by March, 2025

I want to be on the *New York Times Best Sellers List* in 2025 or 2026.

You see, those are specific. Two of those happened within the specific time frame.

The publisher put up money, plans to publish by June. Now, the *New York Times Best Sellers* list is something that I have to make happen. Remember, God helps those who help themselves. Intent is everything. I'm the one who called around when my original publisher blew me off.

INTENT IS EVERYTHING! IT IS POSITIVE ENERGY!!!!!

When I made my intentions known, I did a couple of things that I think really help.

1. I meditated on my desire. I used a Zinc rod in my left and a Copper Rod in my right hand. This is Egyptian in nature, sometimes called Pharaoh rods. Copper is masculine (sun) and Zinc is feminine (moon). It activates your third eye. It completes a circuit. When I meditate, I can feel energy coming up from the ground. These are also very healing.

2. I take about 15 minutes everyday or every other day, just concentrating on that goal.

3. In the meantime, I also make a wish or dream board. Get some cork, paper, and a pen. Put your wishes on it. Put it somewhere that you see often. I'm not sure if it's subconscious or what, but your dreams are kept kinda in the back of your mind, and it also helps to manifest.

If you do these things, I guarantee you will manifest. Keep watch though; sometimes things don't happen the way you think or expect.

One time I asked for a sign of a butterfly, and it appeared in a magazine, not in the air. I didn't even notice at first. Pay attention! I've had friends that made comments about my manifestation that I didn't even notice. I think that is why the time frame is so important.

Keep working on this and in the meantime, remember you are here to make the world a better place. Remember you are trying to ascend, trying to get to 5D. Manifestation is a part of this.

Most of us especially if you are reading this means you are awake and probably what is called a starseed. We have chosen to be here, right now, in this place and on this planet. How exciting!

MORE ON STARSEEDS. CAN YOU BE A STARSEED AND A HYBRID?

Think about it: there are many types of beings that have been introduced to our planet, so of course, it would make sense that you can be more than one. I can't believe no one has mentioned it before now. I've come upon the realization of some of us who are a pleasant blend of more than one starseed type. We are almost like a hybrid. These characteristics are true of certain types of beings. Yes, being a blend is not the same as being just one type.

Here are some of the characteristics that I think help us identify ourselves if we both are Pleiadian and Arcturian or others. Pleiadian blends seem to be fairly common. There are other types out there, but I will be talking more about this blend. Now some differ in functionality and talents.

Yes, it is possible to be both a lightworker and a starseed though. So I believe you can be a mix of these. As for lightworkers, there are many types. They often overlap.

While as many people say there are at least ten types, I believe that either you are lightworker, or you are not. Most lightworkers have an extremely high vibration, are usually living in 4or 5D, are great examples, are kind, compassionate unifers who can manifest and teach great things. Go online and you can find tests to see what kind you are. I bet you are more than one type!

As we get farther into The Age of Aquarius, I am excited to see the positive changes and the love that will be felt by all: starseeds, lightworkers, and all higher vibrational souls. We are at the very beginning of an Age that will last for thousands of years.

Remember to try to do good whenever and remember that what you do affects others in a positive or negative way, always, even in the littlest things.

Here is a list of what they have in common.

1. We never fit in or feel like we belong.
2. You are a healer or a lover of astrology, Reiki, crystals, or other types of energy.
3. You give off high amounts of energy.
4. You are neurodivergent in some way.
5. Intensely Intuitive.
6. Commanding presence.
7. Deep need to help humanity.
8. Empathetic
9. People who need healing gravitate towards them.

10. Deep affinity to Earth and animals.
11. Many talents.
12. Great manifestation
13. Accidentally create jealousy by people who want to be you.
14. Humble, or very gentle.
15. Pacifists
16. Have a hard time understanding why people don't "get it"
17. Can do psychokinesis(Move objects)
18. Very high integrity.
19. Selflessness
20. Super creative
21. Hates hypocrisy and injustice
22. Robust, healthy or larger than average.
23. Interest in learning and education
24. Higher than average IQ.
25. RH negative or carrier.
26. Bores easily.
27. Moves or talks quickly.
28. Appreciated beauty in all things.
29. May struggle with addiction.
30. Odd or metaphysical things continuously happen around them continuously.
31. Able to see through people and situations.
32. Leaders, and know they have been called.

(Notice that these qualities could be considered neurodivirgent?)

Lemurian/Atlantean Starseed: These starseeds are ancient as they come. These come from Earth. They are highly intuitive, great with knowledge both in technology and people skills. They are natural born leaders, healers, often Reiki Masters, yoga, crystal healing and herbalism. They believe in touch for healing and often like to do things physically to help people heal. Both of these starseed often have an affinity for water, Atlanteans more so. I was told by Mark that I am a Lemurian starseed, and it's in my DNA.

Indigo/Crystal/Rainbow Children: These are not really starseeds, but came onto the planet a little differently. They do not think like the majority of the population, are often extremely empathic, want societal change, are compassionate, very astute, intelligent, have a need for freedom, and are usually ambiverts who need their alone time. They are very deep thinkers and feel like they are born with a mission. There have been waves: first the Indigo, then Crystal and then Rainbow. Yes, they are all different, but all similar at the same time. They are here to bring change. I feel that many autistic children are crystal and rainbow children. These children are so advanced, and such an old soul! Never happy with the status quo, and always initiating change.

Pleiadian, Mintaken and Vegan Starseeds: All three of these starseeds are loving, peaceable, and believe in harmony and are healers. Mintakens are very much into crystals and astrology. Pleiadians tend to be super creative and artsy.

Lyran, Sirian and Hadarian Starseeds: Both possess ancient wisdom and great psychic ability. Hadarians concentrate especially on unconditional love, and Sirians also have affinity for animals and their care.

Polarian Starseeds: These beings care deeply for the Earth and its care. They are often mediators and have telepathic abilities.

Andromedan Starseeds: These people love freedom and hate authority but are kind and help with injustice.

Orion Starseeds: These people are truth seekers, ans have an affinity for justice and fairness.

Draconian Starseeds: These are the leader that everyone follows. They exude leadership, kindness and strength.

Arcturian: Arturians are of advanced intelligence and technology. They are probably the most advanced with exceptional psychic ability.

Lightworker: These are not starseeds, so they didn't come from another planet or galaxy. Their souls who have chosen to come to help. That is their mission. While they are of higher vibration, and spread light and healing, they are not necessarily aliens.

2024 TO 2040 WILL BLOW OUR MINDS

I've said this many times to all of you, and it is still literally an open book. But I will say one more thing for you to think about, contemplate, or do with what you have. The next chapters need to be written. It's up to you on what you want to do with it.

Some things to think about;

1. Try keeping your vibration as high as possible. Do you think it's any coincidence that those in power are trying to make us afraid? They are trying to lower the vibration. This is their means of controlling us. Be unafraid, and they have no power.
2. We are a piece of Source, and therefore, can create. What do you want to create? Your reality is up to you!
3. Love will win! Love truly is the answer.
4. You will not always live in 5D, but try anyways.

Remember, we are all evolving and trying to live in Christ-Consciousness. I will leave you with this thought right Now. It will continue and blow our minds! We are just at the beginning. Welcome to the Age of Aquarius! I send you hope, and above all, love.

YES, WE HAVE CONTACT.
Remember: If it doesn't promote love, it will crumble upon itself in the Age of Aquarius.
Blessings to you. Make it Great Day, and
How can YOU Make this World a Better Place?

About the Author

Lana Duncan-Hartgraves is a multifaceted spiritual guide, **author, educator, artist, illustrator, Reiki Master, Herbalist, Hypnotist, gardener and Farm Owner** dedicated to helping others awaken their inner wisdom.

A psychic medium and channeler, she communicates with **Guides, Angels, and Pleiadians**, offering insights that bridge the earthly and the cosmic. With a background in therapy and two master's degrees, Lana brings a deep understanding of trauma-informed ancestral healing and spiritual growth.

Born and raised in Wisconsin with **roots in a farm family**, Lana's upbringing instilled in her a strong connection to the land, nature's rhythms, and the wisdom of generations past.

Lana currently lives on a **small hobby farm in Wisconsin with her family**, where she cares for her **horses, chickens, dogs, and cats**. She integrates her love for animals and nature with her spiritual practices, bringing balance and harmony to all aspects of her life.

With **over 31 years of teaching experience**, Lana has guided countless students, helping them expand their minds and embrace personal growth. Her ability to blend education with spirituality allows her to make complex metaphysical concepts accessible and practical.

Writing under the pen name **L. Duncan Hartgraves**, she has authored works spanning fiction, art, and dream exploration. As an **accomplished artist and illustrator**, she has brought stories to life through her creative works, blending visual and spiritual storytelling in unique and inspiring ways.

Lana's mission is to guide others through their spiritual awakenings with love, authenticity, and wisdom, helping them connect with their higher selves and navigate their destiny paths.